LOCAL

LOCAL

A Memoir

JESSICA MACHADO

Little
a

Published by Little A, New York

www.apub.com

Amazon, the Amazon logo, and Little A are trademarks of Amazon.com, Inc., or its
affiliates.

ISBN-13: 9781542027328 (hardcover)
ISBN-13: 9781542027335 (paperback)
ISBN-13: 9781542027311 (digital)

Cover design and illustration by Holly Ovenden

Author's Note: This is a work of nonfiction. The events that took place are told to
the best of my recollection, and the names and personal details of a few individuals
depicted herein have been changed in order to respect and preserve their privacy.

Printed in the United States of America

First edition

For my 'ohana and the little pockets of mana wahine that have kept me supported, heard, safe.

Kaua'i

Ni'ihau

O'ahu

Moloka'i

Lāna'i

Maui

Kaho'olawe

PACIFIC OCEAN

Hawai'i

0 _____ 80 miles

0 _____ 80 kilometers

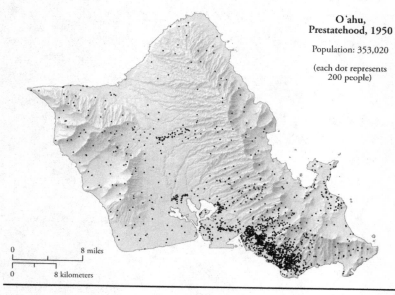

**O'ahu,
Prestatehood, 1950**

Population: 353,020

(each dot represents
200 people)

0   8 miles

0   8 kilometers

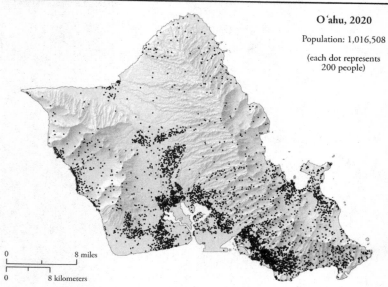

O'ahu, 2020

Population: 1,016,508

(each dot represents
200 people)

0   8 miles

0   8 kilometers

Prologue

American History was a requirement at my Honolulu high school—a private institution founded by missionaries on what was once native Kanaka Maoli farmland. Hawaiian Studies, though, was an elective.

Still, I signed up for a Hawaiian Studies semester in my junior year. The teacher was haole, not from Hawai'i, a catchall social studies instructor who was nice enough but who didn't stray from the textbook and a basic timeline, often presented in a matter-of-fact tone: Captain Cook "discovered" Hawai'i; soon, American missionaries followed, spreading the word of our savior Jesus Christ; then came the immigrants from Asia, Portugal, and Puerto Rico looking for a "better life" with sugar plantation work; then *skip skip gloss gloss* ahead to the overthrow of the Hawaiian monarchy and the annexation of Hawai'i to the United States, our nation superior, home of the free.

We didn't spend much time talking about the way Native Hawaiians—whom we never referred to by their indigenous names of Kānaka Maoli or Kānaka 'Ōiwi—lived prior to Westerners' arrival. We did not leave the classroom to wander into the back of Mānoa Valley, with its rain forest and waterfalls, and study how the land, the 'āina, was at the center of Kanaka spirituality. Our teacher's instruction was given through a settler lens, failing to connect the historical dots to our everyday lives—most of us were the great-grandchildren of those plantation workers who were not rewarded with stability and a living wage but who instead toiled under strenuous conditions and lived in unsanitary camps; our parents had been born in an illegally US-occupied territory, not a peacefully annexed US state. Our class didn't discuss what the overthrow meant for the Kānaka, nor did we study how being stripped of our land, culture, and national sovereignty still affects those of us with Hawaiian ancestry. No one stood up in my classroom and questioned the havoc colonialism, including the missionaries who had founded schools like ours, had wrought on the land and locals. I didn't stand up, either. I didn't ask questions.

Taking Hawaiian Studies showed that I'd had some interest in understanding the history of where I lived and what my Kanaka Maoli ancestors had been through. But back then, at age sixteen, I didn't probe much beyond the bullet points needed to pass tests and get a good grade. I didn't get a grasp of the Hawaiian traditions and language that had been kept alive, despite being banned for nearly a century. It wasn't until after I had moved away from Hawai'i, suffered loss, and yearned for aloha that I wanted to better connect to my culture.

Much of the history woven into this book is not something I learned growing up. It's not knowledge I sought out during my adolescence and young adulthood. But in the years since, these histories, traditions, and mo'olelo, or stories, have become important for me to understand who I am. Doing this research, reading the works of local and Kanaka scholars intent on recentering and contextualizing our culture, has been an honor. (See the Further Reading section in the final pages.)

In writing this book, I made sure to use diacritical marks that preserve the subtlety of the Hawaiian language, including the 'okina (the glottal stop seen before the *o* here) and the kahakō (the elongating macron above this *ō*), which we didn't use in our school writing or see much in local media. And while mo'olelo of Hawaiian akua, or gods, vary slightly from family to family and between Polynesian cultures, it was most important t᷒ ⁻ ᵢₙclude moʻolelo written and studied from the Kanaka perspective, as well as histories researched by locals. I wasn't interested in regurgitating the colonialist savior stories of my high school history book. There has been enough of that.

PART ONE

O ke au i kahuli wela ka honua
O ke au i kahuli lole ka lani
O ke au i kuka'iaka ka la.
E ho'omalamalama i ka malama
O ke au o Makali'i ka po
O ka walewale ho'okumu honua ia
O ke kumu o ka lipo, i lipo ai
O ke kumu o ka Po, i po ai
O ka lipolipo, o ka lipolipo
O ka lipo o ka la, o ka lipo o ka po
Po wale ho-'i
Hanau ka po

At the time that turned the heat of the earth, / At the time
when the heavens turned and changed, / At the time when
the light of the sun was subdued / To cause light to break
forth, / At the time of the night of Makalii (winter) / Then
began the slime which established the earth, / The source of
deepest darkness. / Of the depth of darkness, / of the depth

of darkness, / Of the darkness of the sun, / in the depth of night, / It is night, / So was night born.

—the first wā of the Kumulipo, the Hawaiian creation chant, as translated by Queen Liliʻuokalani

Blended

Before there was sunshine that opened up the morning sky, before there were double rainbows bridging the cliffs of the Nā Pali coast, before Maui's white-sand beaches topped travel lists and honu sea turtles dodged snorkel faces, there was darkness. Complete, utter black. Nothing. My Kanaka Maoli ancestors believed the world began with a lack of light.

Only from the dark could life slowly emerge, each layer brighter than the next. From the depths of the ocean floor sprang forth coral ridges, then sea moss and seaweed tangles, before silvery aku could swim with yellow-finned 'ahi beyond the waves. Ocean life was also protected by the tall grasses and shrubs that grew on the 'āina, or land. The leafy coverings of the uhi yam shielded the hāuliuli mackerel gliding along the coast. Sandalwood trees stretched far and wide from the forests to shelter the sperm whales popping above the water's surface. Only once all the fish and birds and mammals were in sync were we, their human descendants, born—each creature and plant and ancestor dependent on one another, intrinsically linked. The Kumulipo is not only a map of our genealogy but our core agreement to the world we were brought into: it's the Kānaka's kuleana, or duty, to respect nature's harmony. This union is our life force.

Even today—millions of years after the creation of the Hawaiian Islands and nearly 250 years after the first foreigners settled in Hawai'i, changing it forever—it's easy to understand how a deep connection to the elements remains at the core of Kanaka spirituality. Visit Waipi'o Valley on the Big Island and witness the luscious layers of Crayola-green vegetation draping the valley's mountains and the rain-fueled waterfalls running down its crevices, nourishing the kalo crops thriving on the plains below. Go even to the center of downtown Honolulu, with its tight blocks of office buildings and condos, and you can see the bluest sky reflected in their mirrored facades. Turn toward the ground and notice the intricate weeds bursting through sidewalk cracks, their perky white flowers nodding hello in the breeze. You can even roll down your window during rush hour on the highway and feel the sun warming you over, calming you down.

But if you really want to understand the symbiotic power of nature and how it's instrumental to Kānaka's being, visit the home of Pele, the creation goddess, in Kīlauea, one of the most active volcanoes in the world. Watching her erupt is nothing short of magnificent. Her aura-red lava bursts into the sky from the Halema'uma'u Crater, crackling like a firework. When her fire lands down the mountainside, it swirls and flows, heavy but graceful, determined to find the ocean. There, it cools and blackens, raising smoke from the water, signaling preparation for new life. In a few years, moss will grow and die on this hardened land, enriching the soil to support new forests that will go on to guard sea life and nourish native species. Observing Pele's path, nothing is a myth or metaphor; you are witnessing the creation of Hawai'i, the power of the 'āina birthing from darkness.

It is hard for me to think about any part of the islands now and not see all that power, all that beauty. But as a kid, living in a suburb outside of Honolulu, several islands and modern distractions away from Pele, I barely noticed any of this stuff. And still, I am Kanaka Maoli. I am Hawai'i born and bred. I am what we call local.

Hurricane Iwa was the first time I realized just how alone my mother and I were. It was 1982, I was five, and my mother was panicked. The power had gone out, and she needed to find the propane lantern. Where was it? Where did my father keep things like that? She rummaged through cupboards in the kitchen, under the sink, past the errant Tupperware, until she came across it in the back-corner cabinet just below the junk drawer. "Now, where'd I put my lighter?" she said, digging through her pockets before pulling it out. Flick, flick, flick. Nothing. The wheel slipped under her finger again and again, her decades of smoking betraying her in this moment of need. It took her five tries to get the flame to hold.

With the power out, there was no familiar hum of the TV, no lazy churn of the ceiling fan to set the pace. All we could hear was the wind picking up outside, batting against the window, trying to get in.

Before heading to the fire station for his twenty-four-hour shift, my father had run masking tape in an asterisk formation across all the windows to prevent them from shattering, a precaution that locals know to take ahead of the one or two big storms that threaten Hawai'i every year. Just like we know to go to Foodland and load up on canned essentials like Spam, Vienna sausages, corned beef—exports brought to the islands during wartime that became breakfast staples, often paired with fried eggs and rice. Locals take these measures out of ritual, not out of fear. We never thought something bad would *actually* happen. Mostly, the storms didn't amount to much.

But Iwa was one of the few that did. Once my mother had the lantern lit, its glow casting eerie shadows on the kitchen island between us, it was unclear what to do next. The winds were getting louder, sounding closer, echoing off the Wai'anae Mountains that our suburb of Makakilo was built on. My mother was a woman keen on keeping her composure—born and raised in Louisiana, she was a "Southern belle," she often joked—and there was a primness and fragility about her that governed her petite frame. She entered rooms with a soft step, did her

9

best to hide her clumsiness, and pouted with her eyes when her feelings were hurt. Looking at her then, the uncertainty on her face, I could tell she was struggling to hold it together. I started to cry. "It's all right," she said. "It's all right." She reached across the counter to touch my arm. My sobs quickened. I was seconds away from a full-blown fit. "Maybe it's best we just go to bed," she said. "Wake up and it will all be over."

"But I don't wanna go to bed," I cry-hiccupped.

She exhaled. "You want to sleep with me tonight?" I looked up at her, nodding and nodding. She turned toward the staircase, my cries softening as we headed up to her room.

I had never slept in my parents' bed before—my mother did not want to form bad habits, even though my father slept at the fire station several nights a week. Their king-size bed felt massive, with a four-poster frame and an open-air rattan canopy decorated with carve-outs of palm leaves. Some summer days, she'd invite me in, and we'd read books and color, reveling in the grand airiness of having nowhere else to be. In those times, the room would feel serene and peaceful. But in the dark, with the storm thumping on the windows, I felt exposed in the huge space. I curled against my mother's side. I felt the shiver of her body as she put her arm around me and pretended to sleep.

That night, I woke up several times to the rattle of the wind, but when morning came, it was, indeed, over. Iwa had left a cracked window in our living room, some fallen trees in the backyard, and our home without electricity for a few days. But that was nothing compared to what could have gone wrong. My father was stationed twelve miles away in the oceanside town of Wai'anae, where some of the most ferocious waves and winds had hit, forcing around a thousand people to evacuate. The storm could have made permanent the rifts that our family had been avoiding for years.

My dad had never been home much, often running his landscaping business when he wasn't at the fire station. And while my mother and I were usually together, we mostly remained in separate spaces, out of each other's sight. My mom, a high school English teacher, tended to hunker down in the living room, grading papers or watching VHS tapes of soap operas that she had recorded. I, an only child, hung out in the so-called family room, conjuring up my own band of female superheroes or lip-syncing to Donna Summer's "Hot Stuff" to an audience of Barbies. In the evenings, I would join her on the couch for a low-maintenance dinner fit for an '80s working mom—microwaved chicken, topped with a sauce from a packet, beside the scoop of rice required for any local meal—served on our lap trays and accompanied by a rundown of which characters were returning from the dead on *General Hospital*. At the roll of the credits, off I was to bed.

My mother never said that she missed my father, nor did she wonder out loud where he was when he wasn't at work; she kept her worries and discomforts to herself.

My father would show up on random afternoons, bringing with him moments of lightness. He didn't have to deal with the day-to-day mundanity of domestic chores and routine. He could come in with a chocolate haupia pie and an offer to help me put on a summer concert (he'd be Billy Ocean to my Boy George), then disappear to his office or go back out to work. It's not like our family suddenly felt less precarious when he was around or that we magically turned into one of those joyful, matching-aloha-print 'ohana that we saw in local ads. There was just a greater feeling of security. He was the one who knew where we kept the lantern.

When I was a little older, in the second or third grade, an island-wide tsunami alarm went off in the middle of the school day. My father picked me up while my mother was on her way home from teaching at the high school. Once back at our house, my father and I climbed up to the roof. We lived at the top of the mountain, six hundred feet above sea level—a thirty-foot wave was not likely to get us, my dad reassured me. "Then what are we doing up here?" I asked. I had never been up on the roof before. It was exciting. The day, like most days in

Hawai'i, was sunny and clear, and from our vantage point, we could see the frontside of the mountain, much of it developed into parceled subdivisions branching out from Makakilo Drive, the main drag. "If it does," my father replied, "we can watch da waves wash everyting away."

The tsunami never came. But I remember thinking how scary and thrilling my dad's proposition was, even though it seemed wrong to sit by and witness the erasure of the Hawai'i we knew. It was a darkness and excitement I could hold, though, because I knew my father would protect me. My mother felt vulnerable to disaster. But disaster didn't seem to ruffle my father. He made it feel like an event.

My dad, Gabriel "Butch" Machado Jr., was a local boy through and through. A mix of Portagee (the jokey, local-ized version of *Portuguese*) and Kanaka Maoli (Native Hawaiian), he had black curly hair, dark-brown skin, a Pidgin cadence, and a lack of airs. He may not have directly preached "mālama ka 'āina," or "care for the land," and he may have preferred a blues guitar to an 'ukulele and a motorcycle to a hike, but he was comfortable with the forces of nature. He understood that the 'āina had been there long before any of us—and would be there long after.

It's an understanding that's woven into the mo'olelo, or stories, we heard growing up in Hawai'i. With her eruptions, the creation goddess Pelehonuamea, better known as Pele, has the power to both form new 'āina and take away the old from those who abuse it. Her fire often rolls into gentrified neighborhoods of the Big Island, unleashing her anger upon the haole, or foreigners, who have developed homes and vacation rentals on sacred land. Her fiery path of destruction often veers away from where locals live, drawing a literal line between those who respect the 'āina and those who do not.

As keiki, we also heard tales from friends of friends about curious kids heading into lava tubes and seeing a womanly figure with long hair warning them to get out. Or about cousins who ran into ghostlike night marchers, those who once protected high-ranking Hawaiian chiefs, on the coastline of Ka'ena Point and around Diamond Head Crater. And while some might call these stories myths, locals know the heart of the message passed down from Kānaka Maoli is true: you don't mess with the 'āina.

But that traditional undercurrent often runs against how we live in modern Hawai'i. O'ahu, the island I grew up on, has a rapidly growing population, currently surpassing one million people, which is about a quarter more than it was in 1980. When I was a kid, my town of Makakilo was a maze of modest tract houses and townhomes, with a single food mart at the bottom of the hill and several churches sprinkled throughout. In recent decades, developers have focused on building gated communities at the highest points on the ridge, with home prices nearing $3 million. Meanwhile, the plains at the bottom of the mountain, Kapolei, were nothing but empty lots when I was young. Now they're home to four shopping centers, a sprawling outdoor mall, a University of Hawai'i campus, an under-construction high-speed transit rail line, a Wet'n'Wild water park, and a five-star Disney resort where you can watch a hula show with your lū'au bento for around $200 per person.

But long before resorts hired underpaid locals to perform a bastardized version of the traditional dance in coconut bras, centuries before foreigners showed up in droves (or at all), Makakilo was the observation tower of the kāhuna. From such heights, these spiritual practitioners could listen to Papa (Earth Mother) and Wākea (Sky Father) in the heavens and relay their messages to the ali'i, the ruling class. The kāhuna would trace the winds and map the stars, advising chiefs on when to plan feasts and guiding voyagers on when to take to the sea. The Kānaka Maoli's entire way of life was aligned with nature. Just as the tides tell you when to set lures for aku, the soil will let you know when it is damp enough to grow kalo, the starchy taro root that was my Kanaka ancestors' greatest sustenance. Kānaka believe the ʻāina is an extension of the human body, and the peaks of Makakilo were there to help them divine that connection.

However, all that changed when British and American colonists started arriving in the late eighteenth century: what they saw in the ʻāina's fertile soil and waterways was a means for economic gain. British naval captain James Cook is believed to be the first European to have extensive contact with the Kānaka, beginning in 1778, and many foreign ships followed within the next ten years. Hawaiʻi became a pit stop on the way to trade fur in China, its forests picked over for coveted sandalwood. While chiefs controlled some of these sandalwood deals with Western traders, exchanging the fragrant ʻiliahi for ammunition and other goods, things quickly got out of hand. Captains and crews needed to eat, taking up resources and leaving the common Kānaka, or makaʻāinana, who cared for the land, hungry. These Western settlers also brought with them diseases—measles, whooping cough, gonorrhea, syphilis, the flu—that annihilated the Hawaiians. In 1804, an epidemic, possibly cholera, was estimated to have left half of the islands' Kanaka population dead.

Before Western contact, up to a million Kānaka Maoli were believed to live in the islands; a century later, only fifty thousand remained.

As makaʻāinana were either sick, starved, or redirected toward tasks for sea captains, the ʻāina also suffered. Crops went unplanted. Fishing nearly stopped. During this time, Chief Kamehameha from the Big Island set out on a decades-long quest to conquer all the Hawaiian Islands, with the intention of unifying them into a sovereign monarchy. The idea, in part, was to protect Hawaiʻi from foreigners trying to stake their claim.

But missionaries started arriving in the 1820s, and it didn't take long for them to make inroads with the aliʻi, converting many in the ruling class to Christianity. Those missionaries became trusted advisers to chiefs and members of the Hawaiian monarchy (including King Kamehameha's favorite wife), pressuring the monarchy to establish a separate legislative body that would outlaw "sinful" cultural rites like the hula and grant outsiders the ability to purchase land—never mind that the Kānaka believed the ʻāina, as both an ancestor and part of their person, wasn't anyone's to own.

In 1848, this group of haole elites got their way: King Kamehameha III, the second son of Kamehameha the Great, pushed through the Great Māhele, establishing the institution of private property in the islands. By this agreement, about a third of the land went to the Hawaiian monarchy and a third to the new government. But the king hoped to protect the makaʻāinana by setting aside the remaining third and giving them two years to purchase it. Despite posted signs, many makaʻāinana weren't aware of or didn't understand the process for buying land—after all, there is no word in the Hawaiian language to describe land ownership. Nor could they have paid the fees in American dollars even if they did understand what was going on; many still lived outside of any set monetary system. As a result, the members of the haole elite were able to swoop in and buy up much of the makaʻāinana's third when the two-year deadline passed.

During this time, Makakilo, the mountain where my home would eventually be, remained mostly abandoned. Instead, prospectors concentrated on the more accessible plains below in Kapolei, which were sold in 1877 to an Irish businessman, James Campbell. He turned it into what would become the economic engine of Hawaiʻi for the better part of a century: a sugar plantation.

Men and women came from China, Japan, Korea, the Azores (where my father's Portuguese ancestors were from), Puerto Rico, and the Philippines to power these plantations. Over the course of a century, more than three hundred thousand workers put in ten hours a day for as little as $3 a month, tearing up the ʻāina to plant, harvest, and export a processed crop that would harm the health of future generations. Meanwhile, Campbell, taking an aliʻi bride, secured his place as one of the wealthiest and most powerful men in Hawaiʻi's history.

Campbell's name still echoes where I grew up: the nearby public high school is named after him, and so is the industrial park where my father owned a landscaping business and plant nursery. Much of my father's work involved dolling up the entrances to other businesses in the park—construction companies, boat suppliers, shippers. In what is perhaps the ripest embodiment of the irony of modern local living, my father provided for his ʻohana by planting native palms to beautify stolen land that the Campbell Estate leased out to him and other local businesses for a dollar a square foot.

But the takeover of Hawaiʻi was not just about land and commerce—the US government had another interest. In 1887, a group of haole elite landowners, accompanied by a militia, held King Kalākaua at gunpoint and forced him to sign the Bayonet Constitution. The "agreement" diminished the monarchy's power, granted foreigners voting rights while instituting land-ownership and literacy restrictions that disenfranchised Kanaka voters, and led to the eventual ceding of Pearl Harbor to the US government for use as a naval base. Although Kalākaua's sister, Queen Liliʻuokalani, took over the throne after his death in 1891, the haole elite had already gained too much power; within two years, she was overthrown in a coup backed by the US military. Before the turn of the century, Hawaiʻi was annexed to the United States, which has since used the islands as a strategic military location between the continent and Asia.

This affected Makakilo, too: once a place for contacting the heavens, its mountains became home to a bunker, housing massive guns and pillboxes in the mid-1900s. Though the bunker was eventually shut down, nearly a dozen military bases remain active around the island. Roads were constructed from Honolulu to access a naval air station near Kapolei post–World War II, which paved the way for housing construction in lower Makakilo. My parents bought their first home there in 1976.

Growing up in Makakilo in the '80s and '90s, all I knew was that the town I lived in was quiet and boring. I hardly noticed the beauty of the mountains I saw from my living room every day, much like the way cornfields become wallpaper to a kid in Iowa. Looking at the Wai'anae mountain range—its soft slopes grazing the clouds, its crags and crevices deep with both ancestral histories and the fertility of bright-green vegetation—it should be impossible not to feel its power, not to understand how the 'āina is the key tenet of my ancestors' spirituality.

But stories of the kāhuna were not the topic of my dinner conversations or taught at my Christian elementary school. For many of us local kids, these histories were buried under the American rituals of homework, fast food, and prime-time television lineups. We knew we lived in one of the most beautiful places on Earth—we could see it from the lanai extending from our homes—but the understanding that we were "lucky we live Hawai'i" was controlled by every sitcom vacation episode that called the islands "paradise" and every tourism commercial that had coined a similar slogan. We were taught to see our homeland the way tourists did: always sunny and uncomplicated, a playground for others.

That's not to say that many local families don't incorporate aloha 'āina, or a love of the land, into their daily practice. There are many Kānaka who raise their hands in a triangle of thanks to Maunakea, the sacred mountain and firstborn child of Papa and Wākea, and who dance the hula, an homage to the wind and the sea, at family gatherings. Appreciation for the papaya that grows in the yard or for the waves that allow a surf session before work are ways many locals keep that tenet alive. But my family was not one to sit in the moment, breathe in the sweetness of the plumeria trees, and let out a long exhale. Like many working and middle-class families, my parents were busy, focused on their work and inner lives. Instead of feeling one with the land, we often felt like islands unto ourselves.

An only child, I can count on two fingers the number of kids who came over to play. My mother wouldn't let me hang out with the neighborhood kids my age ("They're too rough," she said of the siblings who tussled like normal siblings) and didn't like me playing outside, where she couldn't see me. It wasn't until I was almost eight and saw a TV show slumber party that I asked to invite a school friend over for a sleepover.

The first kid to visit was the daughter of a fellow teacher at my mother's school. I showed her my two-story Barbie home, let her be the coveted Peaches 'n Cream doll, and didn't say a word when she rammed the Corvette into my dresser. I was overly concerned about whether she was having a good time. I cannot remember if I had one.

The second was a kid I didn't talk to in my first-grade class but who just magically appeared in my bedroom one day. "I've got a surprise fo' you," my dad said, then brought out a Hawaiian kid named Toby, whose dad worked with mine in some capacity. They had stopped over to take care of some business in my father's office (a place I'd later realize was where he went to smoke weed), leaving Toby and me to . . . I wasn't sure. We chased each other around the house a few times before I just asked him if he wanted to watch TV. We caught half an episode of *The Electric Company* before our dads reappeared and Toby took off.

Most of the time, I just made up my own fun. One of my favorite activities was to act out episodes of an imagined show where the main character was Viva, a superhero whose name I stole from the local milk company. Her getup was a combination of Jem and the Holograms rock-glam during the day and leftover plastic Wonder Woman costume by night. Viva always had an entourage who adored her and a group of lassoed baby dolls whose lives she needed to save. Wherever Viva went, there was adventure and purpose.

When I wasn't rescuing Rainbow Brite or lip-syncing to sassy tunes, I loved to pillage my mother's dresser and drape her blouses over my shoulders. I yelled at my dolls and gave them time-outs in the bathtub, imitating how I believed my mom scolded her students in the classroom. I agreed with her when she said I wasn't sporty because I was clumsy like her. I stuck to the dainty, girlie things she preferred, like piano lessons and ballet. I made good grades and behaved in class, so much so that my kindergarten teacher pulled my mother aside to express her concern over my perfectionism. My mom, upset by this remark, didn't see the problem. She was always so put-together, her hair sprayed and dresses ironed. I was eager to be her mini-me.

Sarah Jean Graves was not a child of the Hawaiian elements. Unlike my father, she was haole, foreign, white. Born and raised in a conservative Baptist family in Shreveport, Louisiana, with an accountant father and a stay-at-home disciplinarian mother, my mom had been brought up to believe a woman should behave a certain way and live by certain rules and standards. Constraint, more than connection, was in her cultural fiber.

Even though she had moved to Hawai'i after college "to get as far away from the South as possible," there were hallmarks of Southern femininity she just couldn't shake. She never left the house without her legs covered in pantyhose to teach public school in Wai'anae, where August temperatures soared into the nineties and the majority Kanaka and Samoan student body practically lived in slippahs. There is no doubt she stuck out like a pale, sore, proper-English-speaking thumb in one of the farthest stretches of O'ahu, where families hoisted the Hawaiian flag from the beds of their trucks. But she loved it there.

In her first few years of teaching at Wai'anae, before she met my father, my mother lived on campus and made fast friendships that she kept until she retired. With the peaks of Kamaile'unu Ridge behind her classroom and the waves breaking outside her windows, she learned that education was a multiway conversation, a place for passion, even fun. She called her students "my kids" and learned to accept that they skipped class when the surf was too good to pass up. She also learned what mattered to *them*. She heard Israel Kamakawiwoʻole, then just a student with a beautiful voice and a heart full of resistance, playing the ʻukulele on the stairs outside of her building. Years after local comedian Andy Bumatai became famous for jokes that embraced the Pidgin language, he sent my mother, the English-grammar nerd, a thank-you note for putting up with him in class.

My mother's days could be difficult. A student once held a knife to her neck. She had to break up lunchtime fights. Teenagers were not inclined to concentrate when temperatures reached the triple digits in classrooms without fans or air-conditioning. But she didn't want to teach anywhere else. She admired that her kids were honest and said what was on their minds, which was not the case where she grew up. And in return, her students embraced her goofy haoleness and corny jokes. Her yearbooks were jammed with notes from her students, with some writing entire pages of loving jabs at her silly humor, compliments on her hip (if modest) style, and comments about how they were happily surprised to have learned anything at all.

How my mom did or did not belong in Hawaiʻi was never something I gave much thought to. She just was who she was. She may have put a lot of effort into her appearance—itself a facade that set her apart—but her love for Hawaiʻi was not put on. What allowed her to adapt was the way her Southern sweetness overlapped with Hawaiian aloha. She had a sunny, easygoing way of talking and an inviting laugh that brought people close. She would chat up the woman behind her in line at the grocery store and commiserate with a salesperson over a rude customer. She was always looking for comrades or conspirators, and finding them was never hard with her giant hazel-gray eyes and sweet-tea demeanor. It was mesmerizing to see her disarm people, winning them over in the most casual way. During chance encounters with coworkers and former students, they greeted her with hugs and local-style double-cheek kisses, telling me how lucky I was to have her as a mother, before joking that I looked nothing like her.

But when it was just the two of us, no one else around, my mother took a break from seeking connection. She would retreat to her couch spot in the living room, where she'd sit, cross legged, with her tray of papers and the remote. It felt like there was a force field around my mother when we were home, that to respect her was to leave her alone. And that only made me yearn to understand and connect with her more.

Whatever exciting lives—whatever local lives—my parents lived outside our suburban home, I didn't know anything about them. I heard about my mother's teaching prowess in her classroom second-hand; my landscaper father never shared his knowledge of palms and fauna, rainwater and sunlight. Perhaps their long workdays left them exhausted and ready to collapse as soon as they pulled up in the driveway. Or maybe they had learned through their own upbringings—my mother in a strict Southern Baptist family, my father with parents who argued constantly—that home was where you shut down and turned inward, not recharged with your 'ohana.

But still, they had certain standards they expected of me, even if they were somewhat contradictory. My parents were both public school educated and barely religious, but they sent me to Christian private schools. My father's tongue was prone to the use of *dat* and *dem*, but my mother corrected me whenever I spoke Pidgin. "It's 'the socks are stinky,' not 'the socks are stink,'" she'd say. My parents wanted me to fit in with those who appeared "refined," who could traverse the Western world with ease, who had a familiar set of Christian morals.

Meanwhile, what was free and right in front of us went unexplored. Makakilo remains one of the greatest places in Hawai'i to view the stars, but my parents and I never sat in the yard or gazed up at the sky. I didn't kick around a ball and never really learned to ride a bike. The brush behind my house was not for hiking. Family trips to the beach were not on the agenda.

I didn't develop a hunger for the intricacies of the 'āina. I was an indoor kid who avoided dirty fingernails and mosquito bites. I wouldn't take the risk to climb a tree or get on a surfboard. I struggled to understand the carefree fun of my classmates who knew which guavas were ripe enough to pick from the playground trees or who were eager to play games like Chinese jacks whether or not they were any good at it. I had to observe and think everything through, only to still hesitate to join in.

Even in my own yard, I wasn't sure what to do. The trade winds were the only noise around, and I was scared of the quiet. I'd learned that silence was where loneliness resonated. So I made noise inside my head—plays, plots, episodes starring Viva, school scenarios reimagined to go my way. I didn't give the 'āina a chance to show me that the sounds of grass rustling and myna birds singing could be a comfort.

The few times I sat in the sand or waded in the ocean as a child were with friends and their families. Once, at Ala Moana Beach Park, my friend Kelly and I had convinced her parents to let us go buy shave ice. We were maybe seven and way too excited to walk the few hundred yards to the concession stand without adult chaperones. Not eager to get back to her parents, we sat down with our cones of brightly colored ice in a grassy area, a road separating us from the sand. A pair of tourists came up and asked to take our picture. "Look at these cute Hawaiian girls," the woman in a wide-brimmed hat giggled to her friend. Kelly was Portagee haole like me, but without the Kanaka part and much fairer. We weren't exactly the postcard version of Hawai'i's multicultural rainbow. We smiled and leaned our heads toward each other in our '80s neon one-pieces, shave ice syrup dripping down our fingers. "Thank you so much," the tourists said as they hurried away. Like many local kids before us, we were memorialized as token Native Hawaiian children in someone's vacation album.

The closest thing I remember to getting beachy with my parents was not a casual day at 'Ewa Beach Park, just a twenty-minute drive from Makakilo, but a legit vacation to the other side of the island on the North Shore. I was eight, and we had only taken a handful of family vacations before—Disneyland, Maui, and once, the South to visit my mother's family, when I was too young to remember. It was a big deal for us to visit a fancy resort. Turtle Bay was not just a hotel; it also had long-term cottages for rent, a pool, a spa, and a golf course, which made it seem more high maka maka than the standard single-building hotels that littered Waikīkī. There were places to walk around and smiley workers in crisp aloha shirts saying "hello-ha" at every turn. My mom had emphasized that it would be nice for the three of us to hang out together—something, for some reason, we couldn't do at home.

Except the vacation didn't end up being a deep bonding experience as a threesome. I spent a good amount of time playing alone in my separate hotel room before my dad dropped by and asked if I wanted to go to the pool.

During car rides to school and running errands, my father wasn't much of a talker. Still, I understood that his way of showing affection was providing things for my pleasure—my favorite radio station, my choice of after-school snack, a Friday night at the mall—and then setting me free among these instant joys.

"You evah had a piña colada?" he asked as soon as we stepped onto the pool's terrace. I shook my head. I followed him to the thatched poolside bar. "A piña colada for me and a virgin one fo' her," he told the bartender. "How's dat?" He smirked as I nodded, big eyed, sucking past the ice chunks stuck in my straw. "So good," I told him.

My father, having done his parenting part, was ready to relax and headed toward the lounge chairs. Until I interrupted him. "Daddy, do you want to see me dive?" My mom had taken me to swimming lessons the past few summers, and I had finally gotten over my fear of the water.

"Sure," he said. I handed him my drink and skipped over to the deep end.

I found a spot far enough from the pool corners and made sure my toes were just over the edge. I bent my knees. I checked the angle of my arms over my head and turned to make sure my dad was looking. When I popped up, my dad was smiling at me. "Good job, girlie," he said. I must have grinned for a whole five minutes.

After some time lying out, my father had another idea. "Follow me," he said. My dad loved playing tourist. If you spent your whole life watching foreigners being treated like gods while you worked to beautify the 'āina for them to enjoy, then being on the receiving end of such pampering would be a reasonable goal. The server being served. But that didn't mean hotels loved locals. Managers tell their employees, who are also locals, to watch out for fellow locals bumming amenities. If you have the brown skin and casual air of a local, you are given the eye when you enter the lobby and make a beeline for the bathroom. You are looked up and down like my father was when we arrived at the rental stand for various types of water equipment.

"We want one of dose bikes," he said, pointing to the red-and-blue plastic contraptions several tourists were pedaling in circles in a buoyed-off section of the ocean.

"Are you a guest of the hotel?" asked the young woman behind the counter, her hair perfectly tucked behind her ear with an orchid.

My father was shirtless, like he often was at home, with a scant patch of black curly hair on his chest, and he was wearing the local '80s uniform of tiny board shorts. "Yup," he said, sliding her his room key.

"Those run twenty-five dollars an hour," she replied.

My father pulled down his sunglasses to meet her eyes. "I guess dat means no kama'āina discount, den, huh, sistah?" he asked.

She shook her head.

"Worth a shot," he replied before telling her to bill the room. He didn't look back.

Since my feet barely reached the pedals, my dad did most of the work. He swerved around tourists, splashing them in the face, perhaps not by accident. He backpedaled to get some waves going, trying to make the 5 mph ride interesting. A few hundred yards away, at the point of the inlet that the resort occupied, locals waited in the surf lineup. Beach access is the law of the Hawaiian land—all beaches are open to the public—but locals can't just waltz into the hotel and jump off the edge of the inlet to catch the soft wave that washes up in front of the hotel gym. Instead, they have to go around the hotel's private property and paddle out over endangered coral to reach the surf point. This is how private landowners get around the beach-access law. While dozens of surfers competed for their thrill, my dad and I, along with a handful of tourists, were in our bubble—the water mostly still, cluttered with clunky machines, my dad showing off for me. I wouldn't have traded it for the world.

My mother never made it out to the beach or pool that day, but the big event for the evening was dinner at a fancy restaurant. She came into my room wearing a hip black jumpsuit with gold knot earrings to get me dolled up, too. But instead of styling me to look cool like her, she pulled my long brown hair into a half pony, brushed my trademark bangs forward in a straight line, and topped it all with a red bow. The new knee-length dress she had bought me for the occasion was a pouf of plaid and ruffles—something more appropriate for a hayride than a dinner overlooking the ocean. At eight, I was already beginning to have my own tastes, and that outfit did not suit them. I was into loud, weird prints and lots of plastic jewelry; a year later, I would chop all my hair off into a "boy cut."

"Next time, can I pick out something?" I asked. She reminded me that I was lucky because little girls don't usually go to dinners like these. I sulked to the elevator, where my dad was waiting.

"You look like . . . a doll," he said, kissing the top of my head.

"See, Mom, this is weird," I whined. She gave me her "shush now" look. My father was wearing his slick going-out outfit, a beige button-down shirt and polyester slacks, his curly hair combed and fluffy, his Tom Selleck mustache on point. Having grown up without money, he enjoyed spending it when he had it—like when a big landscaping job came through—indulging in food, drinks, and an overall good time.

"What a good-looking family," my mom said, admiring the image of us in the elevator mirror. What I saw when I looked at our reflection was how mismatched we were in style, in coloring, in mood. My mom was beaming with her out-of-the-house cheeriness. My dad barely acknowledged her comment before letting out a smirk and turning away from the mirror. I was too busy staring at the two of them, wishing that, for once, they'd look at each other.

At the restaurant, we were shown to our table. The three of us didn't go out to dinner together much, let alone fancy dinners like this where servers tossed salads and lit desserts on fire tableside.

The waiter came by and asked what we would like to drink. "Oooh, I think I'm going to get some bubbly," my mom said. "And she'll have a Shirley Temple," she added, pointing to me. My dad got another piña colada.

"Can I have a piña colada, too?" I looked at my mother.

She gave me her "no" face.

"Pleeease." I stared up at her.

"Give her da piña colada," my dad said to the waiter. "Virgin."

My mom reached for my arm and leaned into my ear. "Be good," she whispered.

"So, a virgin piña colada?" the waiter asked. My mom nodded. "All right, I'll get those and be right back to see if you are interested in any pūpūs," he said.

The three of us buried our heads in our leather-bound menus, our silence punctuated only by the sound of workers setting silverware on the tables around us.

"Oh, look, they have lobster tails," my mom said, trying to break the ice. "What do you think they did with the rest of the bodies? Do you think there are sad lobsters swimming around, wondering where the extra weight went?"

I shook my head. My dad smirked but didn't look up.

"So, I never asked, how was the pool?" she tried.

"We rented one of those bike things," I said. "How come you never came?"

"Oh, that sounds like fun," she said.

I looked over at my dad. "It was, right, Daddy?"

"Yup, we smoked 'em," he said, still looking at his menu.

My mom smiled. "I bet they were just jealous because you guys were so cute."

It was weird to watch my mother, whom strangers found so charming, fail to capture my dad's attention. It was even more uncomfortable to watch her dart her eyes back down in defeat.

When the waiter came back, my mother ordered the pâté for pūpū. "You OK with that?" she asked.

My dad looked at the menu to see what it was. "Sure, why not," he said.

The pâté arrived in a little silver bowl, grayish brown and slightly chunky. My mother coached me to spread it on one of the tiny toasts from the platter it all lay on.

I spread the pâté carefully, trying to prove I deserved to be there, and popped the toast into my mouth. But I could tell something weird was going on: my parents were both staring at me, waiting for a reaction. It was rich and different and yummy, and much like with the piña colada, I immediately went in for seconds. That's when my dad let out his trademark cackle.

"Whaaat?" I asked in a half-whining tone.

"Do you know what dat is?" he said.

"No, you never told me!"

"It's goose livah." He cackled again.

My mom giggled as she took her bite, too. They looked at each other, laughing in sync. To be honest, I wasn't sure what the big deal was—we ate raw fish and pork cheeks; my dad ate quail eggs over sea urchin. But they were laughing together, even if it was at my expense. I couldn't decide if that filled me with relief or made me want to stomp to the bathroom. So I just kept eating.

That dinner was one of the last times the three of us spent more than an hour together.

My parents had always been clear opposites. Even as a kid, their kid, I didn't understand what they had in common. As a teenager, annoyed by everything about them, I found my parents' differences even more puzzling; I could not comprehend how they even hooked up. But it wasn't until my twenties, when I stayed out all hours, boozing, laughing, and messing around, that their pairing made more sense.

Before my parents were strangers passing through my childhood home, they were freewheeling young people in the early '70s. My mom, a Southern bookworm with a blonde flip and steady teaching paycheck; my dad, a working-class braddah who fixed motorcycles and dreamed of opening a shave-ice stand. They were kids in the most chill, luscious place on Earth, in the middle of a counterculture revolution.

They met at a party—depending on whom you asked, my father might have had a girlfriend at the time—and for their first date, they watched Jimi Hendrix and his guitar wail at the Waikiki Shell, an outdoor venue across the street from the infamous beach. Later that summer, my father swept my mother away for a weeklong trip to the Big Island. He put his rusted, gutted VW "love bus"—decorated with a futon and an *Endless Summer* poster—on a ferry, and the two of them drove around the coast, stopping to lie out in the sun and hike through the lushness of Waimea Valley. Of all the pictures I've seen of my mother, my favorite is a Polaroid from this trip, taken mid-hike. She is surrounded by banyan trees, giant sunglasses perched on the top of her head and a pack of cigarettes practically falling out of her shirt pocket. She is looking up at the photographer, my father, a few feet ahead of her, with an expression that says, "I don't know where you're taking me, and that's fine."

My father was a guy who looked like trouble—or at least like he didn't care what people thought. At age thirteen, he'd moved out of his parents' house to live with his bachelor handyman uncle a few streets down. His main objective was doing what he had to do to get others off his back so that he could then do what he wanted. My mother, you could say, followed a similar strategy in her youth—getting straight As allowed her to run about under the radar. According to my father, it was my mother who was the impressive partier, who could stay up chatting and drinking everyone under the table. And yet, she was still a woman raised on tradition. She told my dad when they first started dating—she at twenty-five, he at twenty-three—that he had a year to decide if he wanted to marry her. When the year was up, she asked him again. He answered the same way he had about the pâté: "Sure, why not."

As a young couple with a rebellious streak, they leaned into their differences. My father liked that my mother was smart; he saw her intelligence as a prize—and as an excuse to avoid having to hold any bookish conversations himself. My mother loved that my father was nothing like the football player she'd dated or any of the frat guys she'd known as a sorority sister. In bringing my dad back to Alabama and Louisiana, where people didn't look like him, she got a rise out of her family. My father said they got a kick out of playing up the cultural divide. He'd dress in a paniolo hat with a feather in its brim and bright aloha shirts for dinner, his Pidgin and dark humor on full display.

Telling me that story was about as direct of a conversation as we'd ever have about my parents' "mixed marriage." In 1980s Hawai'i, we didn't talk about race in terms of brown and white. The dichotomy was local versus haole—my mother, haole; my father, absolutely local. But these ideas weren't explored beyond skin tone, birthplace, or state of mind. Just like we were "lucky we live Hawai'i," the messaging from media, both near and wide, was that we were a melting pot. We were supposedly the multicultural, post-racist future the rest of America was striving for. Mixed marriages, like my parents', were simply the norm, and they still are—around half of Hawai'i's population is in an interracial marriage today.

Even as a child, I knew that we lived in a special place, a place that embraced and was infused with many types of people and many ethnic rites. But no one talked about the price our ancestors paid to achieve that blend. In school and at home, over conversations that stayed breezy, we stuck to simple histories of settlers, missionaries, and plantation days to explain how we became one big, harmonious "mixed plate." We didn't think about how accepting these happy-ending narratives without mining them further diminished our ancestors and the 'āina itself.

"No make waves" is a common refrain in Hawai'i. Go with the flow, accept the way things are, no need to ruffle feathers. While I was eager to show aloha, I didn't feel chill. For as long as I could remember, I felt a nagging urge in the pit of my stomach to get out of my reality, my isolation. I may have been technically local, but there were many times, for many reasons, when I didn't feel like I belonged. I had bought into that unrealistic ideal of a local girl—light-brown skin, beachy vibes, impossible to rattle. I was so caught up in this image that I couldn't see that what made us local was actually the nuanced lives and complicated histories right in front of me.

About a year after our Turtle Bay vacation, I noticed my mother in her couch spot, her lap tray pushed aside, the phone in her hand. I was at the top of the dining room stairs, peeking down at her. I saw her pull tissues from the couch crevices and wipe her eyes. After she was done, she quickly stuffed the used tissues back under her. She repeated this same routine again and again. The tears wouldn't stop, no matter how much she dabbed them away. I heard something about "a baby" and "why her." While I had witnessed my mom check out many times, this was the first time I'd ever seen her actually fall apart. And even then, she was doing it in secret, hiding the evidence.

"You wanna watch TV?" I called out to her. She looked at me, startled, then stern.

"Later," she said.

I stood there for a moment, hoping she'd change her mind and invite me over, but her gaze didn't let up. I turned around and walked back to my room. I didn't want to push her away further.

One afternoon several weeks later, she invited me into the master bedroom and sat me down across from her on the floor. We had just come back from one of our biweekly trips to the mall, where she would ask my opinion as she tried on outfits. "I have to tell you something," she said.

She and my father were separating. It didn't mean they loved me any less; they just fell out of love with each other.

My eyes welled up. A weird, long wail rose from my gut and spilled out of my mouth. Even though my mother's words were the furthest thing from a surprise, I couldn't stop the tears, the loud noises, the ragged breathing.

My mom reached out to hug me. "I'm sorry," she said. "I'm sorry. Things are going to be OK." I'd still see them both, and in some ways, not much would change. "It'll be OK," she said again. "I promise." Tears streaked her made-up face.

To nine-year-old me, their split made sense. They did not seem like the lovey-dovey parents on *Growing Pains* or *Family Ties*. I also believed that whatever my dad had chosen to do outside our home, leaving his mail to pile up on the kitchen table for months, must have been more fun than being with us.

But when I think back on that day, I think about how many times my mother probably practiced what she would tell me. I imagine her writing it down, scratching it out, and rewriting it until it felt fool-proof. Then she had to deliver the news alone. My dad, the guy whose very presence could excite me and who could fix physical objects like cars and dolls, could not, would not, take emotional ownership of our family.

I wasn't OK, but I pretended to be. Later that summer, I would have my first full-blown panic attack. My mother thought it'd be good if we left the house to see a matinee. We got ten minutes into some Gene Wilder romp before I started crying hysterically in the half-crowded, pitch-black theater. I believed our house was on fire. I just knew it was. My mother whispered to me that she was sure it was fine. Why wouldn't it be? She told me to calm down and watch the movie. But I couldn't stop crying. I couldn't catch my breath. I was adamant that our home, the one my dad, the fireman, no longer lived in, was in flames. She ushered me out of the theater before I caused a bigger scene.

But the afternoon when she told me the news, we then put away our new clothes and made lunch. I scooted closer to my mom on the couch, until our lap trays touched, but not quite our bodies. She flipped on an old Marilyn Monroe movie where men dressed in drag to get the bombshell's attention. We sniffled between bites of our sandwiches, the commotion over Marilyn drowning out our intermittent tears. She didn't say anything about a baby or another woman, and I didn't ask.

The Power of Shame

When I was about seven, I was up early on a Saturday to watch *Snorks*. I can't remember what I rubbed up on—probably a pillow or couch cushion—but I remember feeling a nice hum between my legs. I sat in that warm tingle, the waiting room to euphoria, enjoying the thrill of my accidental discovery, my own little secret.

I associated the sensation with *Snorks*, a *Smurfs* rip-off set under the sea. I thought something special was going to happen the next time I watched a bunch of googly-eyed creatures with snorkel flutes for heads, and so the next Saturday, I turned on the TV and patiently waited. But nothing happened. By the weekend after, I had forgotten the whole thing and went back to watching cartoons while shoveling Fruity Pebbles into my mouth.

Any lessons around sex, at least by people in authority, were delivered to me in weird, disassociated fragments. My mom gave me a logistical birds-and-bees talk not long after my morning with the Snorks: A woman has a punani, she said, and a man has a . . . I'm not even sure what she called it, but it wasn't *ule*, the Hawaiian word for *penis* (the Hawaiian word for *vagina* is actually *kohe*; *punani* is slang). But the gist was that a man puts his private parts in a woman's punani, and that's how babies are made. "Don't let anyone touch your punani."

This fell in line with the baby-making framework that my Christian elementary school felt mandated to tell us every year: Sex was a means to procreate, a matter for heterosexual, married couples. No one talked about masturbation, not even in hushed tones, and they certainly didn't discuss exploration or female pleasure.

My Christian middle school took it a step further, with my health/ PE teacher—a slimmed-down version of the cliché with a mustache and whistle around his neck—holding a very special class in an extremely somber tone. He brought in a guest, a woman who came with a collection of fetuses in glass jars. There must have been seven or eight of them, one for nearly every month of pregnancy. Some women choose to kill babies like these, she said, passing around the jars, because those women were bad girls who got pregnant too young. The message was clear: don't be a bad girl who gets pregnant, and don't be an even worse girl who has an abortion.

I went home that afternoon grossed out, both by what I saw in the jars and what I perceived to be a hyper-preachy tone. The class reminded me of the one in sixth grade when we watched a three-part series about the devil in rock 'n' roll—the satanic messages in records played backward, the too-sexy thrusting of men in leather pants, the pretty-boy heathens that were Duran Duran. Back then, when I told my mom about the anti-rock doc, she let me come to my own conclusions. But when I mentioned the fetuses floating in formaldehyde, she flipped. Anger was a rare emotion for her; tempers belonged to my father and, later, me. But on that day, she saw red. "What was the name of this teacher? What did he say? Where was this fetus woman from?" She called it propaganda and said that my body was my choice. "Still, though, don't let anyone touch your punani."

My dad, who had me on the weekends after their separation, offered his own version of sex ed: When I was sixteen, he sat me down in his bedroom and popped in a VHS tape of an episode of *The Jenny Jones Show* in which the guests were mouthy pregnant teens and their equally yelly parents. He then walked out, and I watched the episode alone. We never had a follow-up discussion. My mother and I didn't talk much more about the repercussions of sex, either, until I was almost eighteen and had my first serious boyfriend. In fact, she didn't even ask me if I was having sex. She just made me a gynecological appointment and tagged along, asking the doctor to tell me my options about the pill. I walked out with a prescription for Ortho Tri-Cyclen.

But the funny thing was, despite all the authoritarian messaging pushing abstinence until marriage, nearly every night, my mother and I cozied up to counterprogramming. Nine times out of ten, sex was the end goal in any soap-opera plot, and it often had little to do with making a baby. Subplots of bad business deals and health scares aside, the true appeal of my mother's soaps, even though we never said it aloud, was the sexual tension between two attractive characters. The whole point was to watch a pair of beautiful people overcome a zillion obstacles—stolen kisses on balconies, in closets, in closed-door offices; enemies turned lovers, coworkers turned lovers, once-thought-family-members turned lovers—until they finally lay down on satin sheets, stared into each other's eyes, and passionately kissed before the scene cut away to a commercial break. When the show returned, the characters would have the sheets strategically tucked around them while he talked to her lovingly and she cuddled into his side. The sex itself was over, and the act was still a mystery.

My mother and I bonded over our favorite characters, like Frisco and Felicia's will-they-or-won't-they tension that led to sex, then years of challenges and roadblocks, before a walk down the aisle—which was quite the opposite of the order of events laid out by my Christian school teachings. This hour on the couch before bed was often the most time I spent with my mother all day, my head on her lap or her feet in mine, both of us snacking on miniature Snickers. "Laura is too good for Luke," she'd confide in me, "but there is still something so sexy about him." We hated when a new character captured the attention of an already-paired-up favorite and we had to wait out that new romance until the kismet couple got back together. "They're wasting our time," my mom would say.

I was ten and my half brother was a year old when we finally met for the first time. And even then, it seemed both of my parents would have been fine putting off our meeting indefinitely.

When my parents officially separated and I started spending weekends with my father, he'd pick me up from the Makakilo house on Saturday in the late afternoon, and we'd stop at the video store and a drive-through for whatever PG-13 movie and fast-food dinner I wanted. He then drove us back to his plant nursery in Campbell Industrial Park, where I was supposed to believe he was living in a trailer. He would open the door with one hand and reach for a broom with the other, quickly sweeping out the coating of red dirt that had gathered since he'd last been there. We unpacked our bags of Jack in the Box or Pioneer Chicken and sat on barstools in the kitchen, where the only items in the cupboards were a jar of unopened mayonnaise and a can of pork and beans. Since the living room was empty but for an old love seat left over from my parents' marriage, we'd sit on his bed and play Life and Yahtzee before popping the video into the VHS player and falling asleep.

In other words, it was clear my father spent zero time in that trailer, but I never said anything.

In the morning, he would often run out and grab us breakfast donuts, so when he was gone one Sunday when I woke up, I assumed that's where he went.

Bored, I flipped on the TV, but without any reception or an antenna, the only thing I could make out between the wavy lines was a Road Runner cartoon. It was a hard show to get into since you knew from the start that Wile E. Coyote was doomed to fail in his pursuit of the speedy bird. I turned it off. I got dressed. I brushed my teeth. I opened an empty kitchen cabinet, closed it, then paced around the counter. I sat back down on the bed and waited. And waited.

An hour or so later, the trailer door slammed. My dad entered without a pink donut box, looking like he had seen a ghost. "I have something to tell you," he said. "You have a brother. And he and his mom are on their way ovah."

I barely had time to say "huh" before there was a quick knock and there they were, standing in the small bedroom with us. "Hi, I'm Shellee," said a tall blonde woman carrying a baby on her hip. "And this is Marshal." I looked her up and down. She was dressed in a cutoff tee, shorts, and dirty white sneakers; she didn't wear a lick of makeup. She was a tomboy to my mother's femme. She was also ten years younger than her.

She said she had heard all about me. "Your dad always brags about how smart you are." She said she heard I liked to read—what books did I like? And what a cute pink top I had on! As she kept talking, I nodded and gave one-word answers. I knew, immediately, I was supposed to hate Shellee for my mother's sake, but she was actually very breezy and likable with her warm giggle. Her baby, my brother, had adorable little curls and long eyelashes. Not to mention, this was the most interesting thing to ever have happened to me. A real-life soap-opera moment.

That's when Shellee lifted her crop top and started feeding Marshal. I stood there, eyes wide, before it dawned on me to avert them. I had never seen a bare adult breast before; my mother always changed with the door shut. As she repositioned her nipple and his mouth, Shellee kept talking, asking me what cartoons I liked, how big my doll collection was. Meanwhile, my dad wandered in and out of the bedroom, doing his best invisibility routine. As soon as Shellee pulled her top back down, my father reappeared and said we had to go. He had to get me back to my mother's.

My dad opened the door for all of us to exit. Shellee turned around in the doorway to face me. She put one hand on my shoulder, smiled with her green eyes, and pulled me in for a hug. When she let go, my dad wrapped his arm around my shoulders and ushered me to his truck. He opened my passenger door and quickly waved to Shellee and his son before driving off.

On the way back to my mother's house, he cranked up the volume of my favorite soundtrack, *Footloose*, drowning out any possibility for conversation. I wanted to ask so many questions (*Is this why you left? Is this the woman my mother has been whispering about? Do you love them?*), but the answers all seemed obvious. I didn't think to make him have to say it all out loud.

Instead, I reminded him that I hadn't had any breakfast. At the bottom of the hill, we stopped at the sole store in Makakilo. By the time my dad had pulled out his wallet to pay the cashier, I had a box of a dozen powdered donuts, two bottles of chocolate milk, several packets of stickers, and some windup toy lined up in front of the register. He paid for them all without a flinch.

I'm not entirely sure what went down between the time my dad left the trailer and then abruptly spilled the beans that morning. No one ever explained it to me.

I'd eventually learn that my dad had been living with Shellee since my parents split, but my mom did not want me over at Shellee's house until their divorce was final, hence the trailer facade. My mother requested this one display of respect.

To say my mom liked to keep up appearances is an understatement. What I saw in our home was a woman trying really hard to keep it together. She got up and walked out the door with a smile on every day, ready to perform for the outside world, then hid behind her bedroom door when she couldn't keep it up anymore. I didn't understand back then how much it was ingrained in her to tamp down hurt and shame.

All those years of putting on the perfect face before leaving our home, she was hiding a secret, one that even my father did not know, one that she took to her grave: while in college, she had given up a child for adoption.

My mother got pregnant in 1965 in Baton Rouge, Louisiana, a time and place where abortions were illegal. They were mostly only available for wealthy women in back-alley offices—or performed by pregnant women by shoving a tool into their own cervixes. Even if my mother had wanted to keep her baby, Southern society did not allow for an unwed woman to do so, or else she would be shunned forevermore as a whore and her child labeled a bastard. In other words, the only option for my white, middle-class mother was to hide her pregnancy and then give up her baby.

I'll never know exactly how it went down, but from what I've pieced together from talking to her friends and family and from the stories of the more than one million women between World War II and *Roe* who were sent away to maternity homes, it went something like this: When my mother was in her final year at Louisiana State University, she got knocked up. The few people who were around at this time, or who later found out, each have a different theory regarding who did it. There was talk of the football boyfriend, of a fling with her father's friend, of a "Mexican guy," of rape. No one would comment further. I remain unsure if their hypotheses were based on what my mother had told them or stories they'd made up themselves.

For the final months of my mother's pregnancy, her parents hid her away in a maternity home for "fallen women" who, at the end of nine months, were coerced into surrendering their children. There were two hundred such homes across the country in the 1950s and '60s, often run by Christian organizations. These homes were motivated not just by religious values but also by business—the demand for adoptable babies grew after the war.

My mother went to a maternity home in Mississippi, a state away from the gossip that could spread among neighbors, friends, and class-mates. She likely walked through the front door of the Jackson facility and was given a new identity. All the girls in the home were white. Of this, I am certain. In the Jim Crow stronghold that was '60s Mississippi,

Black women didn't get the luxury of hiding their sin and then returning, ashamed, to upstanding society.

In that home, my mother waited. She did what little there was to do. Knitting, sewing, polishing glasses, setting and clearing tables, ladylike stuff. When she wanted to go outside, she put on a disguise, like a wig and a tent-size dress, the exact opposite of camouflage. If she was lucky, maybe there was an excursion to the bowling alley, where the employees were discreet. Like me, my mother was a daddy's girl; her father came to visit a few times. Her mother, though, did not.

Eventually, after minutes and hours and weeks and months and paces and cross-stitches, my mother gave birth. There are stories of women from these homes, deep in labor, dropped off at the hospital door, left to check themselves in alone. There were women who did not understand why the nurse shaved their pubic hair or why, after being given an epidural, they couldn't feel anything from the waist down. Some believed they gave birth through the anus because no one had educated these women on pregnancy or birth or sex or their bodies. Their bodies had never been considered their own to explore and make choices about.

After my mother's baby was born, the nurse might have whisked the crying, squirming little guy away for good. My mother may have never gotten to hold him. She might not have wanted to. Or she may have nursed him for days before he was abruptly taken from her, never to be spoken of again.

These were the truths of how women like my mother were treated: Get in the car and drive back to your old life. Ignore the empty, swollen belly where a baby used to be. Forget the pain between your legs, the clots of blood that stain the clothes that no longer fit. My mother was supposed to go back to being Sarah, the cheerful, charismatic high achiever. But she would never shake the woman who had been forced to hide away.

When my mother found out about my dad having a child outside of their marriage, I wonder what went through her mind. Did she think, *We must keep this from Jessica because it is shameful?* Did she hope that Shellee and her baby would eventually disappear, like she had to? Did she think about the unfairness of how she was punished while this woman who did the same was allowed to live her life as she chose?

Or did she just feel the pain of knowing she'd done everything she was supposed to—finish college, get a job, buy a home, make a life, be a good wife, birth a "legitimate" child, all while keeping her hair and makeup intact—and yet she had failed once again.

What I do know is that after my parents split up, my mother spent more time smoking on the lanai and less time watching soaps with me in the evenings. She was stern about 8:00 p.m. bedtimes and eager to retreat. While I was at my dad's, she went on dates with a physics teacher from her school, a macho ex-navy man who was also freshly divorced. They were married within a year of my parents' separation.

As a teenager, I once asked her if she would have stayed with my dad had he chosen her over Shellee. She said yes. I was surprised and, frankly, disappointed. My mother seemed to love her new husband, despite his flaws. I thought maybe she was just saying yes because she thought that was what I wanted to hear, which made me more annoyed because all I could think was, *Why would you stay with a man who crushed and humiliated you like that, who always seemed so disinterested?*

"I thought marriage was forever," she told me.

Leʻa, like most words in the Hawaiian language, cannot be confined to a single meaning. "Sexual pleasure," "orgasm," "joy"—these are a few options. Leʻa is both comfort and fun; guilt and shame have no part. Unlike my mother's soap operas that skipped over the good stuff, leʻa was expressed openly in mele and hula, with blunt lyrics about genitalia moving up and down and double entendres about moist ferns and stiff sticks. My Kanaka ancestors had a sense of humor about their reciprocal relationships with nature, enjoyment, and each other. Sexual euphoria wasn't just personal, and it definitely wasn't to be hidden; it was celebrated by the community.

That's not to say that sex in traditional Kanaka culture was a no-strings-attached deal. In the name of keeping the royal bloodline pure, the aliʻi had to abide by certain rules. Officially, procreation was only allowed between fellow aliʻi. And while the culture didn't have marriage in the Western sense, with contracts and expectations of monogamy, there was a ceremony marking the first mating of a high-ranking female aliʻi.

For the makaʻāinana, though, sex and sexuality were mostly absent of any expectations or boundaries. Although *māhū* was shorthand for *gay* when I was growing up, it actually refers to a third gender; the Kānaka were not constrained by the Western demands of the gender binary or the demarcations of sexual orientation. Even aliʻi men, like King Kamehameha and his son Liholiho, took male lovers based on desire and as a method of safe sex (you don't have to worry about tainting a pure bloodline if your partner can't get pregnant). Moe aku, moe mai—or sleeping here, sleeping there—was the way.

Still, intimacy was key in relationships, and pleasure was a mutual experience—something Kānaka were taught was important at a young age. If it is not fun for one person (through coercion or discomfort or force), then do not proceed. Having children with several partners was the norm, and just as my Kanaka ancestors had respect and responsibility for the ʻāina, they also did for the caring of their keiki. Their groups often became one big ʻohana.

Lovely as that all sounds, no culture can or should be painted as a broad-strokes utopia. While Kanaka wāhine, or women, were revered in most ways—getting top billing as creator, sharing in strength and power—there were some traditions that left Kanaka wāhine out. And that inequity, ironically, ended up leaving an opportunity for the missionaries to step into.

The kapu system determined relationships between classes, between people and gods, between people and nature. To break the rules meant angering the gods and inviting possible punishment by death. The subsect ʻai kapu, or sacred eating, forbade women from eating certain foods (pork, bananas) and from dining with men. Kamehameha the Great's favorite wife, Queen Kaʻahumanu, had watched foreign sailors and their wives sit down for meals together and wanted such freedoms, so when Liholiho (Kamehameha II) inherited the throne in 1819, she, along with Liholiho's birth mother and his most trusted chiefs, convinced him to abandon the ʻai kapu; abolishing their traditional religion and class system would also stop rival chiefs from claiming rank, they argued. The plan was as simple as Liholiho showing up to a feast near a Big Island heiau, or sacred worship site, and sitting down at a table full of women. When he started to eat, no gods struck the group down; no punishment descended from on high. And with that, guests proclaimed, "ʻAi noa"— they were free—and messengers were sent to announce the end of kapu.

As expected, chaos erupted. Many wondered if their gods were fake, if their beliefs were nonsense. Many followed the aliʻi, ending worship and destroying heiau; others, though, continued to worship akua like Pele in secret. Four months later, when the first missionaries showed up, so did the prospect of a new savior.

The missionaries looked around and saw mayhem. They asserted themselves as the righteous path forward, convincing the Kānaka of their cultural sins and savage ways and leading them toward their Lord, Jesus Christ. The Kānaka needed to repent. They needed to cover up, be modest, and stop dancing the hula. Marriage would bring structure to the disorderly concept of ʻohana. So would gender roles: men and women would adopt Judeo-Christian definitions of male and female; they would only have sex with the opposite gender—and only in the sanctity of marriage.

Not everyone was so keen on Christianity, though. Before the overthrow of the Hawaiian monarchy in 1893, King Kalākaua, also known as the Merrie Monarch, infused pride back into the hula and mele by holding public performances and paying the dancers and musicians, throwing celebrations at ʻIolani Palace, and preserving in writing the oral traditions handed down from kūpuna. But the haole elite, armed with the righteousness of Jesus Christ, had gained too much political influence. The sons of those first missionaries had become plantation owners and real estate barons, whereas the Kānaka were losing ground. The Kānaka had been not only left out of the land grab of the Great Māhele but also made powerless by the haole-run businesses that now dominated the Hawaiian economy.

Over just two generations, everything that once mattered and fulfilled the Kānaka became less accessible. The Kānaka lived in a place where their ancestors, language, and cultural rites were devalued and criminalized, where they had been pushed out of communal living and into poverty and onto waitlists for small plots of land. In the decades since the overthrow, they have also undergone a health crisis. Unused to the processed foods that became cheaper and easier to attain than the fruits and vegetables that they grew on the ʻāina, Kānaka have suffered from disproportionately higher incidences of asthma, diabetes, obesity, and psychological distress than any other group on the islands. To say the Kānaka were oppressed into a baseline of shame that took a toll on their well-being, both physically and psychically, is an understatement.

Eventually, though, while civil rights activists were fighting to end segregation in the American South and protestors called for an end to the Vietnam War, Native Hawaiian activists also began asking for a stake in what was rightfully theirs. Dubbed the "Hawaiian Renaissance," from the mid-1960s to late '70s, there was a public and proud return to canoe paddling, music making, hula dancing, feather working, speaking Hawaiian, and standing up for the ʻāina.

Perhaps the most remarkable event of this era was the sailing of the Hōkūleʻa. Its 1976 trip to Tahiti reconnected Hawaiians and Polynesians to their seafaring heritage—no one had built or used this type of double-hulled canoe in six hundred years. The Hōkūleʻa had no motor or modern instruments, just a fifteen-person crew sailing into the wind, calculating speed using their knowledge of the trade winds and ocean currents, and navigating direction using the stars, the moon, and the sun. When the canoe touched the beach in Tahiti thirty-four days later, the crew was greeted by seventeen thousand people cheering and rushing into the ocean.

That same year, a group of locals, many of Kanaka descent, left Maui by boat for Kahoʻolawe, the smallest Hawaiian island, which the US military had been using for bombing practice. Their arrival and protest brought attention to land rights at large, and the group, Protect Kahoʻolawe ʻOhana, went on to sue the US Navy for violating environmental regulations. After years of pressure, the Protect Kahoʻolawe ʻOhana eventually won; bombing ceased in 1990, and soon after, the island was returned to the state.

Hula was also more widely taught and publicly appreciated again, and contemporary Hawaiian musicians composed beautiful mele about what they had lost and the challenges they were now facing. The Hawaiian language was brought to the forefront, too. Kamehameha Schools, a private school system that prioritizes students with Kanaka ancestry, finally began offering Hawaiian language classes after decades of punishing students for speaking in their native tongue. In 1978, Hawaiian was recognized as an official language of the state.

It was also during this time that rural Hawaiian communities like Waiʻanae, where my mother would spend twenty-five years teaching and my dad would spend twenty years fighting fires, finally started to see the threat of development. Because this was viewed as an attempt to wipe out Kanaka culture once and for all, it was here—as well as in Waimānalo and other rural areas on the outer islands—that the Hawaiian Movement dug in its roots.

When my mother arrived in Hawaiʻi in 1966, the renaissance was just getting underway. She told me that she moved to Hawaiʻi to get out of the South, and I understood that to mean an escape from bigoted viewpoints, but I didn't understand how personal that oppression was.

She gave up her son in July of 1966, and by the fall, she had a position teaching in Laupāhoehoe on the Big Island. Teaching recruiters gave her a choice: she could teach in an area with predominantly white kids or in an area with local ones. She chose the locals. Two years later, she transferred to Wai'anae.

At the moment my mother was bogged down with shame, she found herself in the midst of those openly trying to break free from theirs. She was surrounded by people who were welcoming and vocal, who didn't pretend to be anything other than what they were, who were celebrating their pride and reckoning with generations of damage brought upon them. And they embraced my mother even though she was a haole lady with a weird accent teaching them literal English— that's how much aloha runs through the cultural lifeline of Hawai'i.

As a kid, I was always jealous of how my mom seemed to love her school. I was also jealous of the attention my mother gave her students, not just inside of the classroom but also as she graded papers and wrote college recommendations from our couch. Being a teacher was her calling, her kuleana. She was at home in Wai'anae. Standing in front of the classroom, cracking jokes, going deep on Emily Dickinson, learning and laughing with her students—this was where she thrived.

Now I see that, in many ways, Wai'anae saved her.

In many ways, I wished I could have been Wai'anae for her.

I wanted to be the recipient of her curiosity, her warmth. I wanted to make the woman who had been devastated by divorce and was constantly drained by performance feel somewhat whole.

I always wanted that. But now I understand that shame was never going to let me.

Becoming Wahine

Like most little girls, I looked to my mother as my primary source of feminine influence for the first ten years of my life. Sure, others seeped in: Wonder Woman with her no-nonsense power, Donna Summer telling men to treat hardworking women right, the local auntie who could render a bully speechless with a sharp jab of her own, my third-grade teacher who squatted down to my eye level to tell me "no worry, beef curry" when I made a mistake. But my mother, in her wrinkle-free blouses and manners for every occasion, as well as her pride in work and kindness, was the pinnacle of what it meant to be a woman—one who held it all together. I wanted to be just like her.

That is, until MTV arrived and changed everything.

Makakilo felt like the last suburb in the country to finally get cable, and it couldn't have come at a more pivotal time in my prepubescence. My mom had just started dating Ed, and one evening, I was left in the care of four of her honor students. These kids were not nerds, though. One had her bangs sprayed to the heavens and her lips attached to her boyfriend, whose dimple was deep enough to bury every romantic hope and dream. The other two were jokesters, amped to be in their teacher's home and have access to snoop around. The girls brushed my long brown hair into a dozen wild ponytails, securing them with their own scrunchies. The boys were freaked out by my giant Barbie head toy, which I used primarily as a makeup canvas, and turned her into a piñata, stringing her up from the sliding door and taking turns swinging at her with a spatula while blindfolded. I happily joined in. At ten years old, I thought they were the coolest people I'd ever met.

Eventually, they got bored of my toys and turned on the TV. Not wanting to seem like a dork, I didn't tell them my mom never let me watch much more than Nickelodeon. Instead, I sat there quietly as they flipped to channel 31. What awaited us was a stream of tousled blondes and brunettes in lacy lingerie parading down a strip-club stage. Their red lips parted ever so slightly, their corseted breasts reaching for the sky, their legs split open like arrows. When the bass buzzed in spurts, stiletto heels hit the floor in sharp, pointed struts. When the guitar squealed, a woman ran her fingers slowly up her thigh, over her red lace panties; another crawled on the floor with each crescendoing note. There were also interludes of male band members on motorcycles, but all I noticed were pole spins and pole thrusts and a woman snapping her own torn pantyhose. This was the sex simulation I'd been waiting for. And the image of women I'd been missing: sexy, striking, commanding.

By the looks on the teenagers' faces in front of me, I would say the reaction to Mötley Crüe's "Girls, Girls, Girls" music video was unanimous. "Holy shit," Dimple said before apologizing for swearing. "Those are some tricks," his girlfriend commented. "Let's see if I can land splits li' dat," she said before thumping on the couch, all of us laughing.

While "Girls, Girls, Girls" provided me a lesson on the adult female form—the only breast I'd seen was Shellee's—it also was a lesson on the power those bodies wielded. To me, it looked like they had men at their mercy. The Crüe were falling over themselves like idiots while these ladies towered above them, cool and in total control, using the band's vulnerabilities against them. To have beauty and confidence and to keep not only the men in the video but the teens sitting next to me riveted—that was what I wanted.

What I did not want was to end up alone on the couch, ignored like my mother.

My mother, I'm sure, did not want such an ending, either, and at that exact moment, she was off capturing the attention of Ed, the only man she'd ever date following the divorce from my father. After a few months of only coming around when I was at my dad's, Ed started showing up after I had gone to bed, too. They would drink Miller Lites and listen to oldies on the radio. Ed was ten years older than my mother, twice divorced, with three grown sons and a granddaughter my age. As my mom would remind me again and again, Ed didn't know anything about girls. He was done raising kids.

Ed was nice enough in the beginning. He was big into teasing—putting on his Clint Eastwood voice to say things like "What are you looking at, punk?" and twisting the skin on my arm in opposite directions, for I'm not sure what reason. My mother seemed most impressed by his physique; he worked out daily and competed in triathlons well into his sixties. Like my father, he was a local Portagee with a mustache, but that is where their similarities ended. My father had a laid-back swag, which extended to spending money without worry and choosing his battles. Ed was a military man, which meant everything had an order and a schedule and a budget. If you broke the rules—like not wiping up the water around the sink—he was quick to anger.

Ed, unlike my father, was also always around.

When my mom married Ed, we moved to a smaller tract home in the middle of Makakilo. For better or worse, our dinners included microwaved vegetables and did not include soap operas. *Jeopardy!* and *Wheel of Fortune* reigned supreme. After dinner, we watched what Ed wanted while my mother cuddled up next to him on the new love seat and giggled at his macho-cowboy persona, like calling her "woman" instead of Sarah. On the one hand, it was nice to see her no longer alone in a sea of sectional sofa, but I also wondered how much of this eyelash-batting shtick was just another facade. And boy, was I jealous that she didn't think she had to humor me with this much attention to keep me around.

In my parents' marriage, the imbalance of compromise was set up long before I recognized it; all I'd ever known was that my dad had too many jobs and was thus allowed to be absent while my mother was the one saddled with the chores of parenthood. But with my mother and Ed, I had a front-row seat to the establishment of their skewed dynamic. There was Ed's golden oldies on the car radio instead of my mother's Journey and the Stones, and his *Matlock* over her *General Hospital* on TV. But my mother also took a sudden interest in lifting weights at his gym and hitting golf balls with him at the range, which made me realize I wasn't sure if she ever had any hobbies outside of shopping before they met. No matter, because this was also the end of our trips to the mall. "Ed says we need to cut back," my mother told me, even though she made her own money. He also insisted that we become Episcopalian, a denomination often described as Catholic-lite and that neither had taken to before. Despite all my Christian education, I hadn't sat in a real church service until they joined the Episcopalian church just before their wedding. Suddenly, I was attending Sunday school and singing hymns about walking as a child of the light—at least until I hit junior high and realized I could just go to my dad's house on Sundays instead.

On Friday nights, even when I was way too old to have a 7:30 bedtime, they'd send me to my room so that they could have a date night. I would read through the teen pop magazines I had stockpiled, studying the way Alyssa Milano perfectly teased her hair, ogling at Johnny Depp's bad-boy stare from *21 Jump Street*. There were newer magazines, too, metal ones with '80s hair rockers like Duff McKagan or whatever band member was cutest (for some reason, it was always the bassist). I would listen to my own radio on low, flipping through the pop and rock stations while they played Frank Sinatra with the volume at level eight, my mother's laugh echoing down the hall. The crush of a beer can punctured the chorus every few songs.

But I spent most of the time in my room thinking about how I could get the hottest guy in my sixth-grade class to notice me. What would it be like to feel his lips on mine, his arms around my waist, to be claimed by someone? Would we hang out with the only other girls who had boyfriends, all of us in front of the auditorium, a herd of touches and whispers and looks for others to walk by and envy? I played out versions of these scenarios—the hot boy kissing my ear, the popular girl giving me a knowing smile—until I fell asleep.

I used to dream about running away. Before we moved into the tract home, while it was being built, my mother, Ed, and I lived in a rented townhouse. Sometimes they would ask me to grab the mail and I would stay out for twenty, thirty, or forty minutes. Once averse to being out-doors, I was becoming eager just to get out.

In the smaller townhome, there was no longer a family room where I could play out my more innocent fantasies, the living room was dom-inated by Ed, and my new bedroom felt claustrophobic. But when I was out on the street, staring at the rows of townhomes with shadowy figures moving past the windows and cars pulling in and out of the lot, there were stories I'd never know, that I could make up. Stories that could maybe pull me into their world. I spied on the neighbors as they shuffled to take out the trash, the teens as they huffed on their way to the car.

On our drives to school, I wanted to tell my mother about how I longed for the cool kids to like me, how I wasn't sure where I fit in, but she had been the popular girl. The cheerleader, the straight-A student, the easy-to-talk-to gal who was nice to everyone. There was no way she would understand. It was easier to pick fights. "Why do you always do what Ed tells you to?" I asked.

"In marriage, you compromise," she said in earnest.

When we turned the corner, I would eye the bus stop from the car window. What if I just hopped on the bus one weekend?

So one Saturday afternoon when I wasn't at my dad's, I kept walking past the mailbox and down Makakilo Drive, pausing at the bus stop before heading toward the bottom of the hill. I had no destination; the idea was just to keep moving before I changed my mind. Maybe if the bus passed, I'd hop on. Maybe I'd meet another kid wandering around looking for fun, too. Maybe he'd be cute.

I imagined my mother running up to me and hugging me tight when I returned, leaving Ed in the doorway.

I looked across the street at the birds aimlessly hopping about in the empty church parking lot, then behind me at the subdivision where our house was being built, a row of identical roofs, each the shade of a faded Easter egg. There wasn't even the stir or sound of construction workers. The only person in sight was a man watering pots of bright-yellow hibiscuses on his lanai. Adventure wasn't lurking here. I turned around so that I'd be home before supper. There had to be other ways to escape.

Sometimes on Saturday nights, I would sneak out of my room to the living room and watch *Headbangers Ball*. I still liked pop stars like Lisa Lisa and Paula Abdul and Prince, who, with their dark hair, brown skin, and ethnic ambiguity, were cool and gorgeous and more familiar to me. I did not want to be blonde or fair like the majority of the hair-metal vixens making eyes at the camera; I just wanted to be noticed in sexy clothes and to have the body and confidence to fill them out. I studied the style of metal groupies—fishnets, leather bralettes, studded biker caps—which was so unlike my mother's modest tastes or the beachy casual of the local kids I saw every day. The women I wanted to emulate were unapologetic, bold, nonconformist. They stood out.

And I was into the music, the whole vibe. Everything about hair metal was pure distraction. The vroom-vroom guitars, the heavy drumbeat, the shrill and shred of a solo that carried you away on a rainbow of pyrotechnics. It was enough to drown out any errant worry, erase any fear of boredom. Add the bright stage lights, the destruction of dressing rooms, the passing of whiskey bottles, the blur of touching and smooching and open-mouth laughter, and even just watching it, I felt like part of the party. I craved another hit, another portal through the television screen to another good time.

Before MTV, adulthood seemed like a one-note path to the mundane: empty bedrooms, closed blinds, polite quietness. Or there was the harmonious ideal of the local 'ohana: The tūtū in her mu'umu'u, flower behind her ear, arms open wide to hug her grandchildren as they ran around the grassy yard in slippahs and board shorts. Uncles drinking Bud from a can. Aunties chatting under the plumeria tree. Cousins and calabash cousins and friends who have been family so long no one remembers they technically aren't related, with a plate in one hand, chopsticks in the other. The 'ohana in perpetual lū'au. Real lū'au, with laulau actually steamed beneath the earth in an imu, and tables filled with aluminum platters of homemade poke, sashimi, chicken long rice, and chow mein noodles with hot mustard. A gathering. An embracing. No one left out of the fold.

All that seemed lovely but unattainable, whereas the adulthood carved out by my parents seemed within reach but unbearably dull. *Headbangers Ball* gave me a different window into what growing up could look like, a path surrounded by so much noise and partying that it was impossible to ever feel alone.

Around this time, I started to ask to spend the night at my best friend's house. Jen and I had been close since the first grade, when her parents moved to Hawai'i from Korea. We were both sheltered only children who were a little shy, a lot obedient, and deeply desperate to be cool. We studied the local culture we saw outside our homes and the American culture we saw on our televisions, trying on the surface cues we noticed and observed. This meant we didn't hike through Keaīwa Heiau Park near her house (we didn't know it existed) or race each other on bikes down the steep hill of her street overlooking Pearl Harbor (Jen didn't know how to ride a bike, either). Instead, we cruised Pearlridge Mall, bought surf stickers at Hawaiian Island Creations to cover our binders, and sat outside of the Fun Factory arcade, checking out public school boys from afar, then turning away if any made eye contact.

Jen's dad, like mine, was never home, and her mom was in and out, busy helping with Jen's aunts' T-shirt stands in Waikīkī's International Market Place. Her mom would peek in on us singing along to Skid Row or strutting around in swimsuits, shake her head, and mutter, "You girls so crazy," then leave us with a bounty of McDonald's. If we were lucky, she would also leave a stray pack of cigarettes behind. There were several afternoons where we would conspicuously run down the street, find a shady tree, and take turns choking on our inhales.

Our parents often dropped us off early at school, giving us another opportunity to act out our dream adult lives. While fellow sixth graders played hopscotch around us, we were building "our apartment" out of plastic milk crates under a mango tree. We scrambled around in our school uniform of sailor-collared shirts and plaid ties, calling out our every move in preparation for our rock-star boyfriends' arrivals—if someone else wasn't there to bear witness, what was the point?

"I'm in that one black bra with jewels on it and the cropped leather jacket from 'Once Bitten Twice Shy,'" I told Jen.

"I'm making Richie kalbi for dinner," Jen called out, referring to Bon Jovi's Richie Sambora.

"Well, hurry up because I have to get in there and cook some rice for Duff," I replied.

When our men finally came over—in my imagination, shirtless in leather vests and spandex—we ate together, cuddled together, talked about our days together. We became not the loose, sexual agents we witnessed in Guns N' Roses videos but the nurturing, traditional sitcom couples we longed for in our own homes. It didn't occur to us that we could be the ones commanding the stage, nailing guitar solos in our leather pants.

Probably the most common image of a Hawaiian woman is that of a navel-baring hula dancer, a smile plastered across her face, her hands gesturing "welcome." She wants to give you a lei, maybe show you to your hotel room and serve you a mai tai. Her lullaby voice is sweet, sedate, as if she has never known anything but sunshine. It can lure you into a nap; if you're lucky, perhaps more.

The simplistic, sexual allures of the Hawaiian woman live on in dashboard hula dolls and movies showing foreigners welcomed to the island by Native women who are just waiting to please and entertain, their gentle gestures the embodiment of exotic femininity. Even growing up in Hawai'i, while most people I knew didn't view brown, smiley women with hair down to their waists as exotic, we did see them as desirable.

In mo'olelo, or traditional Hawaiian stories, though, beauty was not about beachy hair or almond eyes or silk-soft skin, and women were not meant only to be seen or to serve. As Pele scholar ku'ualoha ho'omanawanui notes in *Voices of Fire*, female deities, like Pele and her sisters, were described in relation to nature—her back as straight as a cliff, her face bright as the moon. They were athletes and competitors and had complex inner lives. They scaled rocks and recited the history of the Kauaʻi winds. They were also lokomaikaʻi, or generous, catching ʻopihi when a friend arrived hungry and showing compassion when another was in danger. They had desires and opinions; they weren't sitting around waiting for Prince Charming. Pele could turn down men, or literal pig-men like Kamapuaʻa, and her sisters would have her back, pushing these forceful suitors away.

Women were at the center of Kanaka culture—Pō, the first ancestor who gave birth to darkness, was a woman. Papa, sometimes referred to as Haumea, is the Earth Mother who birthed Pele and her brothers and sisters. Laka gave us the hula to express our histories; Hina, the moon to shine in our dark times. They all worked together out of aloha ʻāina, or love of the land, to mend any harm. What they had was mana wahine, women's power—not to be confused with feminism, which is of Western origin and came much later. Mana wahine is the understanding that women hold a multitude of skills and knowledge; they are resilient; they are a spiritual force. And they are strongest when they support each other.

In moʻolelo and the hula, Pele and her youngest sister, Hiʻiaka, often traversed the land together, aiding other wāhine. There was the woman whose husband beat her, whom the sisters turned into a dog, giving the woman the power to attack and demolish her abuser. But mostly Pele and Hiʻiaka complemented one another—to heal the ʻāina, Pele first wiped it clean with her eruption, and then Hiʻiaka planted fresh life upon it. The sisters knew when to let go and make way for something new.

Pele, being the most well-known deity in Hawaiian moʻolelo, is the one we studied in elementary school. We knew she was powerful, not to be messed with. Her fiery imagery was often connected to anger. I remember coloring pictures of her—her brow set in a scowl, her lips pursed as her face and long hair emerged from behind a volcano spewing lava. She was intimidating without context. But in renderings by Kanaka artists during the Hawaiian Renaissance, she is more intertwined with the elements—strands of her hair are the cracks of the volcano itself; the fire is in her hands. If she is erupting, it is a consequence of disrespect for the ʻāina. I don't remember learning that part, though. Nor do I remember tales about her being backed by her sisters or having mana wahine. In my Christian elementary school, we were lucky to talk about moʻolelo (or "mythology," as it was called) at all.

How I would have loved to hear stories of women banding together to take down predators, share skills, and provide a safe space for each other, especially since we were inundated with Bible passages of men prone to violence or duty. In school, at home, and in front of the television, I was starved for tales of one woman offering, without judgment, what another woman lacked.

What I do remember standing out to me in our school lessons, though, was how Pele's anger ran in contrast to the way girls, local or otherwise, were supposed to act. We were supposed to be mild mannered, smiley, unquestioning. We were to take boys' teasing as a compliment—it meant they liked us!—not tell them to stop. Rage, meanwhile, seemed to be the purview of men: my dad when he was disrespected, my stepdad when he didn't get his way, all dads on all TV shows when they were exasperated by their children after a long day at work. I may not have known exactly why Pele was angry, but I was enthralled. Her fire commanded attention. She was not relegated to silence.

One afternoon in Makakilo, my mom out on an errand, I asked Ed if he ate all the potato chips. I was hungry and standing in their bedroom doorway. He was watching football from bed. "Come here," he told me, his eyes not straying from the game. I walked over to his side of the mattress. "Now, what are you asking me, girl?" he said in his Eastwood voice. His response sounded like a joke, but not being totally sure, I rephrased.

"I mean, are there any chips left? I couldn't find any."

He gave me his troublemaking grin. "Couldn't find any, huh? Get over here." I took a few more steps toward him and he grabbed me, flipped me onto the bed, and began tickling me.

"Stop, stop," I said through tickle-induced laughter. But he kept on, his hands reaching up, farther and farther, past my ribs. "Stop!" I repeated, my voice growing louder as he hovered over me. I knew that what was happening shouldn't have been happening. His fingers kept moving for what felt like minutes, until I kicked his shins and his hands let up, allowing me to wrestle away.

"That's what you get for accusing me of eating all the chips," he said in his tough-guy tone, shooting me one last grin.

I went back into the kitchen to try to find something else to eat, but the more snacks I opened, took a bite of, and put back, the more I felt a gnawing ickiness growing. When my mom got home, I told her what had happened. I said I didn't like the way Ed had tickled me. She looked mortified. She said she would talk to him.

A few minutes later, she asked me to come into their bedroom. Ed still hadn't moved from his position on the bed, but now the mischievousness on his face was replaced with grump. My mom walked over to his side, putting the king-size mattress between us. "Ed didn't mean to make you feel funny, Jessica," she said. "He's used to getting rough with boys. It was all a misunderstanding, wasn't it, Ed?"

She looked over at him. There was a beat of silence.

"Sorry," he uttered.

My mom then looked over at me.

"It's OK," I said, my head tilted toward the carpet.

"I told Ed that you're just coming into your body, so you're going to be sensitive about this stuff."

I looked up at her beside him. "Yeah, I mean, it felt weird," I said. "I asked him to stop."

"He thought you were just saying that because everyone says stop when they're getting tickled," my mom said. "Isn't that right, Ed?"

He nodded.

"Are we all good, then?" my mom asked me.

I looked at her as if to say no—I still wasn't sure what to think—but I nodded anyway. I walked out, leaving them in the room together.

I started hanging out with Shellee more. After the trailer jig was up, my dad would take me over to her house in 'Ewa Beach, about twenty minutes away from Makakilo. Shellee's home was without order. The furniture was a mismatch of hand-me-downs and thrift scores, the kitchen cabinets needed a new coat of paint, and the highchair was splattered with squash-colored spit-up and stale Cheerios. At just over a year old, Marshal needed one eye on him at all times and couldn't clearly express his frustrations outside of grunts, whines, and pointing. There was always a lot going on, and I often wasn't sure what I was supposed to be doing at Shellee's and how I was supposed to busy myself. My dad sometimes just dropped me off and went back to work.

But Shellee never failed to be excited when I walked through the door. Keen to my awkwardness, she made sure to engage. Sometimes that meant jokes about the immediate chaos—Marshal making a smelly poop, the annoying toy that wouldn't shut up. She acted more like an older sister than a stepmother or a babysitter, giving me subtle life tips and telling me stories. Like when she told me about how she was burglarized on a recent night. "If a robber ever comes into your house, always pretend that you're sleeping. Let them take the stuff. They don't want to kill you." Or when her coffee pot broke and she gathered Marshal and me for an emergency run to the Salvation Army. "Coffee is the only way to get through the day, Jessica."

Shellee also had friends who'd come over or whom we'd visit, friends she had made in her twenties when she waited tables and partied in Kailua. There was Denise, the pretty blonde who was house-sitting a beautiful home in 'Āina Haina. The three of us sat in the hot tub while Marshal napped behind the sliding door, and I listened as they gossiped about Denise's older boyfriend. There was Kathleen, who seemed to perpetually be in crisis and whose house we went to once or twice to help with her children so that she could just lie down, but instead she'd spend the afternoon crying to Shellee. And there was Judy, who brought over beers and laughed loudly and always wanted to sit outside or go for a ride. I was less intrigued by the women themselves than I was by their friendships with Shellee. How they all seemed saddled by responsibility yet made room for solace in each other. It wasn't moving mountains or ousting evil men, but it was the mana wahine I didn't know I was searching for.

As the years went on, a few of these women would struggle with more debilitating mental health issues and addictions. Some would come over and do bookkeeping or clean our house for money after my dad's landscaping business took off and we moved to his childhood neighborhood of Kalihi. But Shellee never wavered in her friendships. There were always plenty of laughs and Coronas to go around.

There was a freeness and a blondness to Shellee, much like the women I saw in music videos. But she did not wear the getups or the glam of metal models. She liked animals and dirt and had met my dad when selling him plants. She would help him draw up designs for his clients in his growing landscaping business while he dug up the 'āina to put in irrigation systems. The two of them also had chemistry that was both hard to stare at and hard to turn away from. He looked at her like he wanted her; she looked at him like she loved him. He grabbed her ass when he thought I wasn't looking. She was fun, maybe even a little bit naughty, and that had won my dad. My mom was uptight and distracted, and she had given too much of herself away. I could see why this was the path my father chose.

I started to spend more time at Shellee's for another reason, too: I had a playmate or, more importantly, an ally.

Maybe the fourth or fifth time I went over to her house, I was greeted by a spunky tan kid with a bowl cut. He was standing on the couch, having just watched from the window as my dad and I came up the stairs. "Hi, I'm Kalani," he said, jumping off the couch, all smiles and missing teeth and age-six moxie.

"Hi," I said, not moving away from my dad's side. Kalani was Shellee's kid from her previous marriage, four years younger than me and eager to get to it.

"Let's play," he told me. I looked at my dad, who nodded at me to go on. My play repertoire consisted of lip-syncing to Whitesnake and making my Barbies hump each other; I was nervous about what he'd suggest.

"Do you watch WWF?" he asked.

"Yeah, sometimes."

"Let's wrestle! I'll be Hulk Hogan and you can be Macho Man."

I looked up at my dad again, but before I knew it, I was being charged. We tumbled onto the floor, our limbs flying. He kept trying to hold my arms and legs down, and I had no idea what was happening, so I just kept breaking free and followed his lead, pinning his legs and arms, until I realized I was sitting on him and he was squealing, "OK, OK, you win!"

"Get up, Jes," my dad yelled.

"Oh," I muttered, getting off him.

Shellee was laughing. "You really got 'em, Jes!"

And I did. I won. I won at something I knew nothing about. This had never happened to me before. And Kalani wanted to play again and again, even though I won every time.

Kalani wasn't always there on the weekends because that's when he visited his dad, but I started to go over for dinner some weekdays and spend Sunday nights, just so I would have a buddy.

And for everything Kalani wanted to do—freeze tag, wrestle, hide-and-seek—I had a play suggestion, too. I got Kalani to dress up in a feather boa to sashay down the runaway with me, mimicking dance moves from Madonna. We were very different, with very different interests, but that didn't get in our way. We quickly formed a trust that we would follow each other.

The 'Ewa Beach house was down the street from the ocean. Kalani loved to swim; his father, also Portagee Kanaka, was a surfer who grew up in Waimānalo. Even though Kalani was born with a hole in his ear and wasn't supposed to get his head wet, that didn't stop him from running straight into the water.

"C'mon," he told me one afternoon, "catch me." He went splashing in as I stood on the sand. My dad was off running another errand, and Shellee was getting Marshal situated on a beach blanket. I was in my tiger swimsuit, the one that I wore when Jen and I choreographed slithers to power ballads, my bangs freshly sprayed into the perfect wave. I slowly walked in, until it got too deep to keep going. "C'mon," Kalani called again, dog-paddling farther toward the sun. *Why not?* I thought, dunking my head and swimming toward him.

Once I caught up, I grabbed his foot, and I could hear him giggling above the water. I poked my head up, and we were both laughing, the sun catching the drops in our lashes. It was then I realized I didn't know how to tread water. For some reason, in all my swim lessons, it had never been on the docket. I hoped that, just like with wrestling, I could figure this out as we went along.

"Let's go out farther," he said, paddling away from me. I swam a little, then stopped. I was manically moving my arms and legs to stay afloat, to be there, acting like I knew what I was doing. The more I thought about how my movement was all that was keeping me from drowning, the more spastically I kicked and churned the water. I turned around, and Shellee and Marshal looked so far away on the shore. I felt like I was gasping for air, just like I had in the movie theater when I thought the house was on fire.

"I think I'm going to go back in," I told Kalani.

"Awww, why?" he whined, his limbs moving effortlessly in rhythm with the waves. "Let's just swim out a bit more."

I looked at him, so much eagerness in his expression, and told him through gasps that I couldn't. I didn't wait for his response. I took off in a front stroke. As soon as I was on the move, the anxiety subsided. Running was safety.

Being Kanaka, Local, Haole

It happened in eighth-grade biology. Someone finally said it out loud.

My partner and I were about to cut into a frog. I didn't want to be the one to do it. Neither did she. We started joking about throwing up our breakfasts. "I wish I didn't have that *crow-sawnt*," I said.

"That what?" my partner asked. ·

"What what?"

"What did you have?"

"A *crow-sawnt*."

"A croissant?"

"Yeah. That."

"Why do you say it like that? *Crow-sawnt.*"

It was then that Jocelyn, the class loudmouth, turned around from the lab table in front of us to clarify. "She says it like dat cuz she's haole," Jocelyn announced.

I looked up and saw most of the class staring in our direction, laughing. My eyes darted toward the floor. I had no witty comeback, no quick defense. I had been outed as something that didn't feel entirely true. But it hit on something that didn't feel untrue, either.

Clearly, I had learned my French pastry pronunciations from my Southern, haole mother. I didn't go home and tell her about this. Nor did I discuss it with my father, though it would have been a perfect opportunity to talk about what it means to be Portagee in Hawai'i—while we're seen as locals in the islands and our ancestors are from the Azores and not continental Europe, Portuguese are essentially seen as white in the rest of America. In the rest of the world, Portuguese were often the colonizers. Portagee is also one of those ethnicities with the highest rates of intermarriage in Hawai'i; our identity markers had mostly been reduced to bean soup, malasadas, and jokes about being dumb.

Instead of asking any of my questions, I went home and put on Sinéad O'Connor's "Nothing Compares 2 U." I tapped into all the sadness and anger and pain in her voice, shouted the high notes of the chorus, and stared at my thirteen-year-old face in the mirror. I wished I had thick, slippery hair like Jocelyn. I hated that mine had suddenly turned curly during puberty, leaving my bangs a mess and the rest of it fluffy as soon as it touched a brush. I hated the dark circles under my eyes, coveting the smooth skin of many of my local Asian classmates. But most of all, I wanted to feel what I believed everyone else felt—a stronger sense of camaraderie around being local.

My father's paternal lineage can be traced as far back as my great-great-grandfather, Manuel Azevedo Machado, who, at the age of twenty-two, left his family behind in São Jorge, a slender island in the Azores more than a thousand miles off Portugal. It's unclear whether he intended to make Hawai'i his permanent home when he set sail on a whaling ship in 1866 or if, like many whalers en route to Asia back then, he stopped on O'ahu for supplies and decided to stay. Hawai'i was rich in the same green and mountainous landscapes that cloaked his homeland. But the Azores were economically poor and suffering from overpopulation. Educational opportunities were scarce, and social class was essentially determined at birth. Many nineteenth-century Azoreans were eager to find a way out.

Though whaling rarely equated to power and riches and was inherently cruel to the mammals themselves, it was deemed an admirable vocation and a lucrative gamble if a worker was with the right crew on the right boat in the right season; if not, which was more often the case, they signed up for voyage after voyage to pay off the debt they'd accumulated on the previous one. It also wasn't a job for the weak of mind or body; the work involved long stretches of boredom peppered with the massive danger of sneaking up on a multi-thousand-pound creature and harpooning it without drowning your boat or yourself.

By the time Manuel showed up in 1867, Honolulu was already teeming with missionaries, haole businesses, and a harbor lined with brothels and bars. Within a few years, he married a Kanaka woman, Maria Maio, with whom he would have ten kids over the course of twenty years. Not much is known about Maria, but it is possible that her family owned some property because Manuel became a farmer once whaling work dried up in the Pacific. Manuel was one of a small number of Portuguese in Hawai'i when he arrived; ten years later, the Portuguese started arriving by the thousands to work on the sugar plantations. Portuguese made up less than 1 percent of Hawai'i's population in the 1860s; by 1890, they would comprise 14 percent.

The majority of the plantation Portuguese, including my nana's ancestors, also came from the Azores and Madeira Island, workers who had been sold on the dream of a better life in the new land of "Terra Nova." Plantation owners, however, used those aspirations against them. In his book *Pau Hana*, historian and ethnographer Ronald Takaki notes that according to a recruiter for the plantations, the Portuguese were selected to work in the fields because they were humble dopes: they were "sober, honest, industrious and peaceable. Their education and ideas of comfort and social requirements are just low enough to make them contented with the lot of an isolate settler and its attendant provisions."

The Portuguese were just a fraction of the more than four hundred thousand immigrants who would arrive in Hawai'i over the course of the sugar industry's century-long heyday that would shape the islands forever. It all started when a Bostonian, William Hooper, and his mercantile business partners looked at the expanse of wild sugarcane that grew in the wetlands of Kōloa, Kaua'i, down to the beaches of Po'ipū, and realized the Kānaka were sitting on an untapped prize for exportation. Although Kānaka would sometimes chew on the cane and use it for medicinal purposes, they did not refine it. That would be Hooper's enterprise.

In 1835, Hooper and his associates convinced King Kamehameha III to lease them 980 acres of land for $300 a year for fifty years. They were also granted permission to hire maka'āinana. Twenty-three Kānaka came to work on the Kōloa Plantation on its first day, and Hooper put them up in housing and paid them in coupons that could only be used at his plantation store. He envisioned himself as a savior, freeing Natives from what he saw as a feudal system they had been born into. But when these workers started to question why they should trade coupons for canned, imported food when the 'āina, and their lifestyle, could already grant them such sustenance, Hooper deemed the Kanaka workers too troublesome and ungrateful and let them go. He instead recruited a number of Chinese immigrants already living in Kaua'i to work on Kōloa. Hooper wrote to his partners that "a colony of Chinese would probably put the plantation in order," and by 1852—with business booming and plantations opening throughout the islands, thanks in part to the Great Māhele—the first contract laborers from China arrived. Over the next few decades, recruiters brought in the Portuguese, Japanese, Puerto Ricans, Koreans, and Filipinos, too.

The idea behind recruiting groups of workers from various countries was to pit the nationalities against each other to achieve greater productivity and control. Asian immigrants were rarely allowed to move up and become luna, or managers. The Portuguese, on the other hand, were sometimes offered that opportunity, a position that sandwiched them directly between the white owners and the Asian immigrants.

Owners also instituted the "race pride" program, posting each nationality's aggregate attendance and timekeeping records every morning. They also worked with home governments, motivating workers through nationalism and incentives, like requesting that a Japanese social club give talks on the importance of employer loyalty in exchange for plantation owners financing Japanese-language schools on the islands.

Plantation camps were often kept segregated by nationality, and living conditions, though generally crowded and unsanitary, also demonstrated a hierarchy; ditches that serviced toilets in the owner's mansion ran down to the Filipino camp, as one worker documented. But despite segregation efforts, groups slowly began sharing food and entertainment—Japanese would swap musubi for Portuguese sweet rolls, and workers of different nationalities would lay out their prospective lunches like a buffet. Many workers had taken wives, whom they had either brought with them (the Portuguese were allowed this benefit; the Chinese were not) or who were shipped in as "picture brides" to encourage bachelors to settle down. These new families began intermingling. As English became the official plantation language, laborers started to converse more with one another in a hybrid, which eventually became its own language—Pidgin, the language of locals—in Hawai'i.

The tension the plantation owners tried to create between their laborers eventually worked against them—workers grew less interested in beefing with each other and more interested in banding together to strike against their bosses. In 1946, the year my father was born, the immigrant nationalities eventually merged unions, gained employment rights, and unified as Hawai'i's working class.

Local identity formed as a result of this solidarity: the dichotomy of us (the Chinese, Japanese, Korean, Portuguese, Puerto Rican, and Filipino workers) versus them (the haole plantation owners).

Not long after immigrant workers made their stand, sugar production in Hawai'i slowed. The United States could import cheaper sugar from Cuba, and Hawai'i's economic focus began to turn to tourism.

Before Hawai'i's annexation, many workers, at the end of their contracts, escaped on boats to California, where the work and pay were better. But after annexation, Japanese and Korean laborers who had received passports to Hawai'i were suddenly "refused permission to enter the continental territory of the United States" by an executive order by President Roosevelt. Stuck, immigrants were forced to make their way and raise their families in Hawai'i, often moving off plantations to Honolulu to work in commerce, construction, or other odd jobs.

Today, there is no cut-and-dry rubric for what makes someone *local*, though it is loosely defined as someone born and raised in Hawai'i or someone who has lived in Hawai'i long enough to truly, honestly live aloha 'āina. It includes those with familial ties that go back to the plantations, as well as fellow Polynesians (Samoans, Tongans, Tahitians, Māori) and other Pacific Islanders (Fijians) who emigrated to the islands between World War II and statehood as well as in the '60s and '70s. It also includes what we call *local haole*—white people, or people from the continent, who have integrated into the larger community and respect the culture. Ultimately, being local is less about skin color and more about caring for the people and the 'āina.

And yet even within the large umbrella of "locals," unspoken hierarchies still exist. Unlike the Chinese, the Portuguese, and the Kānaka, the Japanese continued to marry mostly within their ethnicity well past World War II. They were the first, outside of haole, to hold government office in Hawai'i. The Filipinos, last to the plantation and paid the least, still hold a large percentage of the islands' manual-labor and frontline-worker jobs. The Kānaka have historically had the highest unemployment and poverty rates—until great numbers of Micronesians emigrated to the islands in the twenty-first century and faced (and continue to face) discrimination because of the scarcity of jobs. Black people, meanwhile, make up a small percentage of the population and are often associated with the military, which comes with its own negative connotations in the islands, on top of the anti-Black sentiment carried over from continental biases. Some Hawaiian activists even warn about the overusage of the term *local* and its ability to hide Kānaka Maoli, their culture, and their fight for sovereignty.

Hawai'i may be the closest thing America has to a melting pot, but with a quarter of all homes owned by nonlocals and an economy dependent on a tourism industry that doesn't always provide a living wage, competition for resources and employment is bound to cause stratification and friction.

One of the most beloved carryovers from the plantation days is the ethnic joke, more commonly known as "jokes" in Hawai'i. Making fun of each other was a way to lighten the mood in the sugarcane fields, or so the story goes. These jokes often set up a situation ("a Hawaiian, a Japanese guy, and a Portagee walk into a bar . . ."), and the punch line is a stereotype embodied: the dumb Portagee, the lazy Hawaiian, or the "chang" or "Pākē" Chinese. While playing up tropes may sound cringey in progressive circles outside of the islands, it's considered an equal-opportunity sport in Hawai'i. No ethnicity is off-limits, and laughing at yourself is part of being local.

I could brush off, or at least roll my eyes at, jokes like "Why did the Portagee sit in the front row of the movie theater?" (Answer: "He wanted to be the first to see the movie!"). I knew I wasn't stupid. But when Jocelyn called me haole, it touched a raw spot—it was confirmation that people saw me as *not* one of them. And yet to her, her joke was probably just a familiar way to get a laugh. (It also underscored how haole I was for not being able to take the joke.)

And yet as light as these jokes are meant to be, harp on any belief long enough, and it can't help but seep into the collective consciousness as truth. Generalizations like "don't piss off Korean moms; they're scary," or "always hire Filipinos because they're hard workers," express sentiments that stem from the race pitting of the plantation days and contribute to tensions, economics, and unemployment rates today. And like all reductive stereotypes, they can become self-fulfilling prophecies. I remember once being at a dinner with my father and several of Shellee's wealthier relatives from the continent. Conversation flowed from the president and his economic policies to religion and other current events. My father didn't say a word. When Shellee's brother-in-law asked him what he thought, he grinned and shrugged. "What do I know—I'm just a dumb Portagee." His answer took me aback. I knew my dad was using the stereotype as an excuse not to talk about things that didn't interest him. But I still wondered how much he really believed he wasn't as intelligent as the educated haole. He had more street smarts and common sense than anyone else I knew.

While my dad often referred to himself as a Portagee, his relationship with being Kanaka was less straightforward. ʻŌlelo, or Hawaiian language, hadn't been passed down to my grandfather or father, and it was banned from being taught while they were in school. Many Portuguese people in the early twentieth century, like my grandfather, still straddled that luna line of hoping for social mobility through white proximity while ultimately being working-class locals—perhaps my papa believed it was best to downplay our Kanaka side. My father, however, was a young adult during the Hawaiian Renaissance, when there was a return to cultural practices and a reawakening of Hawaiian pride. But since he was raised to barely acknowledge being Kanaka (it wasn't even on his birth certificate, nor did my parents put it on mine), suddenly claiming ownership of our Native heritage without being more active in it felt fraudulent.

By the time I was a teenager, Kanaka pride was celebrated loud and proud. The Merrie Monarch hula competition was a prime-time television event. My sophomore year in high school, 1993, marked the centennial of the overthrow of the Hawaiian monarchy, which included a fifteen-thousand-person march to 'Iolani Palace. Sovereignty activists like Haunani-Kay Trask routinely made the news, saying things like, "We will die as Hawaiians; we will never be Americans." I didn't take any political stance as a teen, but it was clear that the Kānaka had an important voice. This was their home; they were connected to it; they belonged. I thought that part of my ancestry was very cool. But if my dad didn't emphasize it, then how could I?

When I was in sixth grade, my mom asked me if I wanted to apply for Kamehameha, a low-cost private school for Kanaka children subsidized by the trust of ali'i Bernice Pauahi Pākī Bishop. It would take some finagling, my mom said, but we could prove my Kanaka ancestry through other relatives' birth certificates. I considered it—the campus was gorgeous and close to my grandparents' house. But I was afraid I wouldn't feel Hawaiian enough once I got there. Would I stick out like a sore thumb among my Kanaka classmates? Were there pieces of the history and culture that everyone but me would already know? Shouldn't I be able to switch between Hawaiian and English more fluidly? It didn't dawn on me that there were many words and cultural stories I already knew because they were woven into local life. It also didn't occur to me that one of the goals of Kamehameha was for Kanaka kids to get back in touch with the aspects of the culture we had lost. I decided not to apply.

I chose Mid-Pacific Institute, founded by missionaries and best known for being the school kids attended when they couldn't get into the "smart" ones, like Punahou or 'Iolani. My best friend, Jen, was going there, and that seemed like a good enough reason for me to go, too.

Around the time I started middle school at Mid-Pac, my father returned to his roots. He moved his new family—myself included, the two days a week I lived with him—out of 'Ewa Beach and into his childhood neighborhood of Kalihi to be closer to his parents. My father's family goes back generations upon generations in Kalihi Valley. They are so deeply rooted in the neighborhood that there is even a Machado Street, named after an ancestor.

While I didn't see my grandparents often when my parents were married, that changed after my nana was diagnosed with Alzheimer's and my dad was stringing together his responsibilities. He decided to rebuild Uncle Mano's single-story home into a two-story house, where we would live above Uncle Mano to help my grandparents, who lived next door. My dad did much of the demolition, design, and build himself, giving me the bay window I'd asked for and Shellee the fireplace she'd always wanted, even though the weather rarely dropped below seventy degrees.

The inside of my father's house was much different than my mother's. For a start, it had as many as eight people roaming around on any given day. By the time we moved in, my nana was already pretty far gone. She was up at all hours, keeping Papa busy and cranky. Several mornings a week, Papa would walk her up our stairs, open the toddler gate for Nana to walk through, then turn around and head home. It was our turn.

"Hi, Betty," Shellee called out from behind a skillet of pancakes. Nana looked up, startled by her name, not entirely sure who we all were, and then took a dirty tissue from her pocket and wiped the surface of the TV. My nana was an anxious woman and had an impossible time sitting still. She shuffled to the screen door, jiggled the handle without any luck of getting it open, and then turned to the other end of the living room and went to the sliding door that led out to the balcony to do the same. She did this in circles again and again. All she knew, it seemed, was that she wanted out.

These mornings when she was with us, we were all getting ready for school or watching Saturday morning cartoons. There was the breakfast slinging on top of the chaos of getting two boys dressed and brushed and hustled to the car. When my dad was there, he would take us to school, leaving Shellee with Nana. Other times, Nana came along for the ride, fussing with the seat belt, her eyes both panicked and dulled.

It was sad to watch my nana become a shell of herself. A retired manager of the local version of Walmart, she, like my mom, had always been put together, with polyester blouses and beautiful jade jewelry, her hair jet black. And now here she was with her roots showing, her shrunken frame drowning in her clothes. Shellee tried to dye her hair for her, but the color was too brown, turning the salt-and-pepper crown of her head a burnt red.

Adding to this chaos, we lived on the main drag of Kalihi Street, where ambulances and police cars sped through at all hours, our dog barking at each and every siren. Kalihi wasn't the kind of neighborhood where kids played outside and you knocked on your neighbor's door for a cup of shoyu. Yards weren't much of a thing, as many families had extended their homes to the property line to accommodate relatives coming in from overseas or to make space for second and third generations moving back in with kids of their own, like we did. No one was chilling on sidewalks or street corners, but there was the hushed chatter of which cars were primarily used for dealing and smoking ice. When Shellee would worry about the abandoned cars, drug activity, or what might be domestic violence going on across the street, my dad warned her not to call the cops. "Do not get involved. Don't be a narc," he said.

But there wasn't ever a time I felt scared in Kalihi. Sure, Kalihi was not Kahala or Hawai'i Kai or Mānoa, where many of my wealthier private school classmates lived. Kalihi was scrappy. But it was also a valley surrounded by mountains. To the north was a less vibrant green hillside with public housing, and to the south, a steeper slope of deep green with houses planted among the undergrowth. There may have been a whole ten feet of leftover property between our home and our chain-link fence, but there was still room for an avocado tree and a lime bush and hedges of the flame-colored croton. My landscaper father couldn't help himself, and neither could the rich soil of the ʻāina, eager to support any vegetation.

I liked being in my father's house, where the communal spaces felt nothing like the stillness of my mother's living room in Makakilo. Shellee was always around, sipping from her Corona while she made dinner, the rush of Led Zeppelin playing from the kitchen radio. She was always up for a chat whenever I pulled up a stool at the kitchen island, one of us making sure to help Nana retie her pants that she kept untying, leaving them to fall around her hips. It was in this kitchen that Kalani and I cleaned the dishes every night, discussing which annoying *Full House* character would win in a fight—Stephanie Tanner or Kimmy Gibbler—while Nana stood next to the counter, wiping the same spot again and again. Marshal, now a toddler, would run up and playfully swat at us in a failed attempt to get us to hang out with him.

As time went on, things would calm down, and people retreated to their own spaces and minds. Nana became more sedate, until she was hospitalized and passed. Papa stayed mostly in his own home, engrossed in ESPN, except for the occasional Sunday dinner of my dad's poke pūpū and Shellee's enchiladas at Uncle Mano's downstairs table. Kalani went back and forth to his dad's in Waimānalo and started to make his own friends at a nearby Catholic school, where as soon as the bell rang, neighborhood boys went looking for fights. I, meanwhile, made plans to go to the mall or movies, several miles away in town, with friends. Otherwise, I was in my room, deep in my fantasies about hanging with the cool kids and rowdy boys or spinning around to INXS and Bell Biv DeVoe—anything that felt like a release.

None of it was a Norman Rockwell painting. But being at my dad's was the closest thing I'd ever had to ʻohana.

Since it was "in town," my dad's house also had the added perk of being close to my new school. Mid-Pac was in the heart of Mānoa Valley, an upper-middle-class neighborhood that was predominantly local Japanese and local haole, which was reflected in the school's student body. I may not have been aware of the plantation-day ethnic wars while I was in middle school, but I was definitely aware of the hierarchies within Mid-Pac's halls by the time Jocelyn called me out in biology.

The popular girls were nearly all local Japanese and all knew each other from the nearby elementary school. Jocelyn was part of the jocks, many of whom were also local Japanese. Then there was the local haole clique, boys who were surfers and troublemakers, who scrounged for money during lunch even though their parents were doctors and lawyers. Then there were small cliques of mixed kids, like my friends and me: the Japanese haole; the Korean Chinese; the Portuguese Filipino Korean Hawaiian; the Korean whose family pretended to be Japanese when they lived in Japan; and my old pal Jen, whose mother was Korean and father was Italian Japanese. We weren't dorks, but we weren't cool, either. We were just there. It was up to us to make something out of it.

When Jocelyn called me haole, it was a wake-up call: I had to figure out how to define myself before others did it for me. I wasn't simply worried about the haole-versus-local question, but the more general adolescent question, *Who the hell am I?* I had always held back and tried to figure out how not to upset others. I waited until I understood my place before making any sort of move, which is how I approached entering Mid-Pac. I watched which girls had the most confidence, the most put-together style, and the most attention from boys. How terribly I desired to be best friends with the popular Sheries and Stacies.

But it wasn't like the Sheries and I had any of the same interests. They were covering their bags in Kerokerokeroppi stickers and listening to sappy pop. I was stuffing my bra and begging my dad to take me to a Winger concert. Still, I got excited when one of them would pass me a note in Spanish class or speak five words to me when we were partners for a history assignment.

I bought all the Sheries and Stacies Christmas presents that first year—little Hello Kitty knickknacks wrapped and tied with silver bows—but I didn't get any in return. I fantasized about talking to the most popular guy in school, until he caught me touching my arm hair, which was getting thicker and darker by the day, and joked to our entire class that I was masturbating. The boy everyone knew as "the hornball" was always making sexual innuendos that seemed to delight the girls, but when a group of us had lined up by the door one day, waiting for the bell, he reached over and grabbed my punani, making a tickling motion for everyone to see. Again, they all laughed.

And so, slowly, I started to wonder why I had wanted to be part of this group at all.

Through middle school and into high school, my little group of mixed pals came together through burn books and invites into each other's homes. At Melanie's, we talked about the hotness of Sean Tanaka's skater bangs as her hippie haole mom made us honey pancakes and her hippie local dad aligned our energies with sound waves. At Farrah's, we choreographed routines for our rap group while her sisters argued with their Buddhist mother about whether to get a Christmas tree. But mostly, we tried to get our parents to leave us alone to figure out who we were. We had them drop us off at heavy-metal concerts, haunted houses, and artsy-fartsy movies. We bodyboarded into tiny waves at Waiks, squirted each other with Super Soakers at Ala Moana Beach Park, and played pool with the public school boys who ran tables at Hawaiian Brian's.

Then there were the moments when we didn't try to be anything at all. One afternoon, I sat with three of my friends on a grassy hill near the campus entrance, as we often did after school, chatting and eating our vending-machine scores. My back was toward the slope, and suddenly, I leaned too far back—before I knew it, I started rolling down the hill, my body flipping in a perpetual somersault, screaming "ahhhh" until I hit the bottom. I looked up at my friends, embarrassed; their faces were a mixture of concern and attempts to conceal their laughter. "Are you OK?" Farrah called down to me. "That looked like it hurt."

The thought of how ridiculous I must've looked made me crack up. I couldn't stop laughing. "I dunno, that was actually kinda fun?" I said, still chuckling as I walked back up the hill.

"It definitely looked hilarious," Melanie said.

"My cousins and I used to roll down the hill behind their house in Hilo," said Becca. "It was awesome." Then she lay down on the grass parallel to the expanse of the hill, crossed her arms over her chest, and started rolling. "Wheeee," she laughed as she went down.

"Dammit, I'm going to do this, too, aren't I?" said Melanie before following Becca's lead.

One after another, then side by side, we all tumbled down the slope, free, feeling the earth's solidity under our backs, our sides, and our chests, our heads dizzy in delight. We were whirlwinds of giggles and grassy bodies, paying little mind to the students passing by on the pavement around us.

It was in these tiny moments that I started to notice what I already had: friends who were eager to take a journey together, who cared if one another were OK.

By sophomore year, even if we were all still figuring out who we were, we'd come to a firm conclusion about what we were not. We were decidedly not the Sheries and definitely not the surfer haole who roamed the halls. So we took those differences to the extreme. To shout to the world that I'd no longer blend in with my upper-middle-class classmates with their Billabong tees and designer bags, I bought obnoxiously bright-colored disco polyester shirts from Goodwill and paired them with knee-high patent leather boots. I painted my rusty, decade-old Buick with suns, rainbows, and peace signs, finishing it off with a note above the brake lights that read "No cherries allowed"—a nod to what we called the Sheries because they labeled everything basic that they liked "cherry." Our teen-angst-meets-aloha mobile had Hole's *Live Through This* blasting from my childhood boom box, and in the high school parking lot, it stood out from the brand-new Acura Integras with expensive sound systems, their subwoofers bumping to Jodeci and Mariah Carey. I had shifted into a full-blown '90s alt kid—a thing that might have been extremely regular on the continent but felt downright exotic in the pop-Jawaiian stretches of Hawai'i. A rebellion not just from my high maka maka surroundings but from this idea of "local" that I felt shut out from.

But my growing give-a-shit attitude extended beyond my outfits and ride. In English class, I piped up when we talked about outsider characters in literature, like Hester Prynne in *The Scarlet Letter* and Atticus Finch in *To Kill a Mockingbird*. "We live in a society that doesn't care if you're a good or caring person—what matters most is if you conform!" I shouted to a mostly sleepy classroom. I was big on calling people followers and joined the school newspaper to write editorials about parking-lot privileges and the new "revolutionary" radio station that probably no one but my friends and me cared about.

Besides being mixed, besides trying to find small ways to break free from the private school bubble our parents had padded around us, there was something else my hapa friends and I had in common: we were latchkey kids. If my friends' parents weren't divorced like mine, then they were busy leading double lives in other countries. Several of my first-generation friends had dads who were often gone on business to Japan or Korea for months at a time while their moms ran their own stores and hustles.

My friend Becca had freer rein than the rest of us. Her mom worked nights at a Korean bar, and her dad had retired from the military and moved back to the Big Island, where much of his family was. Becca introduced our friends and me to guys who went to the all-boys school in her neighborhood and pointed out the stores in the mall that didn't have cameras so that we could pocket tank tops and hair accessories. Some Saturdays, we sat at the hotel pool where her mom's boyfriend was a manager, drinking strawberry daiquiris and ranking the hotness of the cabana boys.

While all our parents tried to rein us in with rules and curfews, they didn't seem to question why we chose underage clubs over the beach or even the mall anymore. The length of their leashes was dictated by how busy their schedules were.

When we told our parents we were staying at the house of a friend they'd never met—because they'd asked, but we assumed they'd never call—we stayed out all night playing pool; wandering Waikīkī; and loitering at the local chain diner, Zippy's, well after we'd finished our 2:00 a.m. eggs and rice. When we said we were going to the movies, we went to a warehouse rave by the docks or sat on swings in Makiki Park, drinking beer with boys we'd met the weekend before.

But between those moments of sneaking around and pushing boundaries, those softer times remained, of just being together like we were on the grassy hill. Heading over to Farrah's after school, our heads touching on the carpet as we ate Gardetto's and judged videos on MTV. Spending the night at Melanie's and making waves with our bodies on her waterbed, rolling out toward the edges, then in toward the middle, giggling at who could churn up the tidal wave. Sitting on Becca's balcony, our feet up, sodas in hand, making up stories about the people who walked by below. I loved being in the spaces of these other girls, our own cozy nooks of mana wahine. It wasn't uncommon for me to overstay, preferring our little intimacies to the chaos of Kalihi and the solitude of Makakilo. "I no like that girl spraying hairspray right next to you while you eat"; "Your haole friend with the weird car, did she eat all our snacks from Costco?"—these are the things my friends would tell me, years later, that their parents had said. At the time, though, they didn't mention anything to me. I was always invited back.

Boiling Point

Like most teen girls, I fashioned my penchant for nonconforming as a rebellion against my mother, who was the poster child for polite femininity. She gasped when I cut the sides of my long hair up to my ears and bleached them with Sun In. She persuaded me to at least consider going to my school formals. It brought me such pleasure to shove in her face that I was OK not doing what everyone expected me to do.

"You're so boring, Mom. Like, when was the last time you actually changed your hairstyle?"

She looked at me with a pout in her eyes, her shoulders hunched. "What's wrong with my hair?"

"It's, like, short, old-lady hair," I told her.

She touched the layers of her curly bob. "Well, when you get old, it's not right to have long hair anymore."

"Says who, Mom?" I rolled my eyes. "That's so dumb."

Conversations like this were ordinary at my mom's house. I'd poke at her to get a reaction, only for her to go back to talking about dinner or the television. By this time, Ed had retired from teaching, leaving him more time to nitpick about crumbs and tiny stains on the carpet. Otherwise, the two of us didn't strike up much conversation. While I lived primarily with my mom and Ed through middle school, by the time I was in high school, I started asking to spend more and more nights at my dad's until I found myself packing up the rest of my clothes one day during sophomore year. The move was less a conversation than an understanding.

"It just makes more sense that I stay in Kalihi because it's closer to school," I said, just to say something.

While my mother's eyes telegraphed sadness, her words let me know she understood. "If that's what you want," she told me.

I nodded. "It just makes more sense," I repeated.

I started to see her on the weekends, but not the entire weekend because that would cut too much into my friend time. My mom and I went on lunch dates, meeting halfway at a seafood joint, Monterey Bay Canners, at the Pearlridge mall. Unlike our sprawling hours in the same house, in different rooms, doing our own thing, for this hour-and-a-half meal, our attention was focused mostly on each other. My mom did her upbeat best to ask about my literature class, share a little bit of her school gossip, and fill me in on the soaps. We often indulged, ordering the stuffed mushroom appetizer, then a sandwich each, and always a dessert, too. We were ladies who lunched, who kept things light—a scenario I could tell my mom enjoyed. And for the most part, I did, too, this hanging out, woman to young woman.

Sometimes, we took a stroll through Liberty House, our favorite local department store, for old times' sake, but rarely did we buy anything. She likely didn't want to upset Ed's budget as much as she didn't want to get into a fight about my clothing choices. Sometimes, we couldn't help but fall back into easy habits: she'd make a comment about my too-thin eyebrows; I'd call her a prude for judging some customer's cleavage-baring outfit. But by this point, she had mostly stopped reacting to my screams for attention, like pulling into the parking lot blasting Rage Against the Machine's "Killing in the Name," which included the lyrics "Fuck you, I won't do what you tell me," repeated about a dozen times. She'd resolved to wait inside the restaurant for me in our regular booth. I'd find her coiffed and bloused, enjoying her iced tea,

surrounded by as many open sugar packets as she liked, in her preferred
Southern belle state of pleasance.

It wasn't that my dad understood any better how to parent a teenage
daughter. He was only around intermittently. His method was not one
of steady guidance but of pointed instruction and interrogation. One
summer, he insisted I work at his plant nursery. It was time I toughen
up and actually work to earn money, not just spend his, he said. So several days a week, I put on my old gym shoes and got in his truck, and we
went down to Campbell Industrial Park. One day, he walked me over to
a cluster of potted palms and told me to work my way to the back of the
lot, watering and pulling weeds. I was the sulkiest of teens, huffing with
every drop of sweat that ran down my temples and grunting with every
yank of the hose that kept getting caught around tree trunks because
I couldn't even be bothered to look at what I was doing. I spent the
entire afternoon waiting for it to be over. I counted the pots I watered,
looked ahead to how many more rows I had left until I was done. It
was so quiet—the only noises were the semitrucks chugging by outside
the gate and the constant sigh of "this sucks" replaying in my mind.

I didn't even make it to the end of the summer. One afternoon, I
fell down a hole and scraped up the back of my leg. It hurt, but it also
looked worse than it felt. I ran to my dad's office, amping up the tears
as I approached him. He rolled his eyes and bandaged up my leg. From
then on, he let me do paperwork instead.

There were other times he didn't let me off so easily. Because he was
a man of efficiency, he would gather up snippets of my life from Shellee
and other parents, which he would then use to discipline me during the
fifteen minutes he was home before I went to bed. He once marched
into my room and demanded I admit to where I went three Saturdays
ago. He had pictures. One of my friends' dads had shown them to him.

There was a party with boys and drinks in red plastic cups. I denied and denied, until I realized he wasn't leaving my room until I admitted something—"You can't bullshit a bullshitter, Jessica!"—so I racked my mind for what he could possibly be talking about and said I went to a house party with some McKinley High School boys. My dad grounded me for two weeks. I later found out that I was not in the pictures of the party he was referring to. That weekend, I had already been grounded for something else.

Sometimes I would talk to Shellee about a guy I liked at school, or she'd catch me staring at a boy in the cologne aisle at Longs Drugs, and two days later, my dad would come into my room after work and accuse me of being boy crazy. I hadn't had a boyfriend, and I didn't even kiss a boy until I was sixteen. It was never clear if the assumption was Shellee's interpretation or his. Did she just want to alert him that high school was a weird, vulnerable time for girls, and his instinct was to shelter me through yelling and intimidation? Except as I got older and grew bolder, his all-knowing fear-mongering strategy—which applied to what I did outside of the house as well as chores I didn't do at home—worked less and less.

"Did you just throw a pile of rubbish on top dat?" my dad yelled as I walked out of the kitchen, pointing to the full trash can.

"Yeah, it was already full."

He looked at me. "Do you just think the magic rubbish man is gonna come and do something about it? Are you dat spoiled?"

"Everyone else fills up the trash! Marshal, Kalani, Shellee. Talk to them!"

"Right now, I'm not talking to dem!"

"Well, maybe you should."

That's when the "listen, girlie" came. The dead-serious eyes. The guttural "knock off the tone." And the thing that drove me mad: "Don't talk to me like I'm one of your dumbass friends."

"You would never be one of my friends. And they're not dumb!" I stomped off to my bedroom. Kalani and Marshal, who had been peeking out from their room, cleared the hallway as the two of us came charging through.

"Don't you walk away from me!" my dad called out.

I slammed the door.

He opened it, popping his head in. "I get da last word!" he screamed, then slammed it again.

"No, you don't!" I yelled out the now-open door, down the hallway, then slammed it one more time.

We'd go on and on like this until I got my phone privileges or my car keys taken away. Even though I knew he would ultimately have the final say, I was pumped up by the spar—the pushing back, standing up for myself, soliciting a response. I loved the way the fire roiled up from my belly, through my chest. I loved the strain in my throat upon release. Pele could burn everything down, assured something new would appear in the wake of her fury, and I could scream at my dad and guarantee this man who was barely around would come back for more. It was a source of both comfort and pride. "You're the only one who can hold your own with him," Shellee once told me.

But I would be remiss if I didn't say that there were other times I was not proud of my anger. One afternoon, Kalani and I were playing Uno on the bottom bunk of his bed when Marshal, then five, kept coming in and messing with our pile of cards. "Teeheeee," he giggled as he ran up and swiped his hand across the discard pile, scattering primary colors all over the mattress. Then he'd dart away, running all of two feet before staring at us like he wanted us to chase him. "Marshal, stop!" Kalani and I both yelled again and again. By the fourth time, he just went for it and jumped in the middle of the game. I grabbed him by the neck and, in some deranged wrestling move, banged his head—once, twice, three times—into what I thought was the mattress.

Marshal and I didn't usually play rough. When he was a toddler, we played Pepé Le Pew, with him kissing me all over and me eating up his sweet little "I love you" voice. Otherwise, I mostly ignored him, my pesky baby brother who always got what he wanted from his still-married parents. The roughhousing stuff was Kalani's domain: Marshal started something, Kalani finished it, and Marshal ran crying to Shellee. But there I was, my hand on his neck, Marshal screaming. Until I looked at his face and saw it was bleeding. I hadn't just hit his head on the mattress but also on the metal bed frame, and he'd gashed his eyebrow. "Oh my god," I screamed. Shellee came running in, saw the blood dripping down his eye, and whisked him off to the emergency room.

I was in shock. "I didn't mean to. I didn't mean to," I kept saying. It was true: I didn't mean to make him bleed. I didn't mean to hurt his soft, sweet face. I definitely didn't mean to act like a monster. But I did mean to silence the irritation.

The '90s was a good era for pent-up aggression. The first time I saw moshing up close and personal was at an all-ages show for the pop-punk band the Offspring. My friends and I found out about it from the cool radio station that filled Hawai'i's musical void, playing punk, ska, metal, goth, industrial—anything you didn't already hear on the radio dial. Offspring was one of the shows they promoted during this era, many of which took place at an old warehouse along an industrial stretch between Kalihi and Waikīkī. At After Dark, there was the roped-off smoking area in what was essentially the parking lot, as well as the dark, no-frills, no-furniture inside space to see the show. Only a plywood partition on stilts separated the drinkers and us teens.

My friend Terri and I found a place to stand off to the side, close enough to the stage but not directly in the danger zone of the real pit, which mostly consisted of military men with buzz cuts run-stomping and knocking each other around in a circle. Their aggressive display did not interest me as much as moving my own body to the music—the small bounces, the head nods, the feedback ringing in my ears. But when the band played their radio hit "Come Out and Play," everything changed. Energy swelled in the painted-black room, the pit extended out, and the young locals and military guys around me started pushing and jumping into each other, too. Men bumped into me from behind and fell into me from in front. I looked at Terri and she looked at me, and we smiled and bumped the guys back. It was fun to push people, especially people who thought they could push me. I felt like a force, throwing my arms out, keeping people away. At sixteen, the edge of the pit was where I was comfortable with the chaos.

My relationship with intimacy was more complicated. I feared it and yet I craved it. I still wanted to be one of those carefree video vixens who could put it all out there, bring men to their knees, and then walk away. But I also dreamed about nuzzling and coded us-against-the-world stares into each other's eyes, about being with someone who'd always have my back. I had no idea how to get past the first step, though, to do more than capture a guy's interest, to actually allow myself to be touched.

There were the boys who'd meet me in secret and then disappear. The hapa dancer from middle school with the long bangs, a grade older than me and my not-so-secret crush. I'd somehow gotten his number, and we chatted late into the night. He told me he also lived in Makakilo and said he was on his way to find my house, and I waited by my window until I saw him waving outside. We sat on my lawn, talking about music, the streetlight capturing his smile as he flipped his bangs with a toss of his head. But then, after our second meetup where we just chatted and did nothing else, he stopped calling, stopped coming by.

There was the cute guy I met at the pool hall freshman year, who maybe liked my friend first, who told me Asian girls were his type until he realized I lived down the street from him in Kalihi. Like the hapa dancer, he also told me to meet him outside of my house, where he grabbed my hand and complimented my ass, or at least pointed out that I had one. I teased him back, giggled, and looked into his eyes, then quickly away. He said we were "going out," then never called or came by again.

Then there was the guy I flirted with all sophomore year at school, who asked me out on a date over the summer and, over the course of several hours, grew annoyed at the risks I wouldn't take—jumping off the roof into the pool at Punahou school, smoking cigarettes bought at a hole-in-the-wall market in Waikīkī, making out at the top of Tantalus. When he parked the car at the infamous teen kissing spot and jumped into the back seat, I was too nervous to join him. He drove me home in silence, then ignored me for the rest of high school.

Then there were the guys I finally let touch me. In those cases, I was always tipsy. My first kiss was with a stranger, skater vibes, a tad shorter than me. I was sixteen, and he was part of a group an acquaintance had invited me out with, each of us seeming to have a predesignated pairing. We all drove up the windy road to the park of pines at the top of Saint Louis Heights. I could barely make out the face of my dude in the dark, but I could tell he was cute, mixed. We all passed around a fifth of peppermint schnapps until pairs started wandering off and I was left standing next to him alone. His head tilted, mine at the opposite angle, until our lips touched, one tongue rolling around the other's. Then we went right back to being strangers.

Then there was my first boyfriend-ish. I was a senior to his junior. He was a fellow grunge-alt weirdo who wore a chain wallet and Nirvana tees the year after Kurt Cobain's death. He was eager to hang out with me because he could tell I cared about music as much as he did. He asked me to join his friends—a small crew of awkward, pimply metal nerds who liked to wrestle each other—in the park near school. When I finally took him up on his offer, he kissed me, and I kissed him back.

It was fine, I think; I didn't remember much after a steady stream of Zimas. He showed up outside of my English class the following Monday, assuming we were a couple. I wasn't sure I liked him in that way; he was a little too in my face, too into me. Even though being adored was all I thought I ever wanted, when I saw his eyes so excited to see mine, him skipping beside me as we walked out of the English building together, I picked up my pace. I had the urge to make a sharp turn toward the campus exit. But I stayed. I went along with it. All of it—the public affection in the cafeteria, the meeting of his parents, the fooling around while they were at work, the invitations to constantly hang out. Part of me felt like I had to. I was seventeen. I had to get a relationship under my belt.

Plus, I knew he was moving in three months. Three months, I calculated, was a commitment I could make without thinking too hard about what I actually wanted.

No matter what generation of local you belonged to, no matter what you were into, if you were a teen in Honolulu, the adventure was out in Waikīkī. Kalākaua Avenue was the central stomping ground for young folks to check each other out on Saturday nights. You could come from the leeward side, you could come around the corner on Kapahulu, you could be broke or live in a high-rise; it didn't matter. The playing field was mostly level—it was literally two flat miles of hotels built over a swamp—for horny local kids just to walk back and forth and be seen. There were skaters, surfers, jocks, and alt kids like me who were excited just to be part of any action. Between all the glances and catcalls, street performers sang Hawaiian melodies, smatterings of older locals went to dinner and a movie, and Japanese tourists shuffled by. But we barely noticed them. Our eyes were on our own people, our own age, our focus on the potential all this energy could bring.

But while the game on Kalākaua Avenue may have appeared even, there were other factors to consider. Waikīkī was created for tourists—we were on their turf. The rows of hotels, fancy shops, and marketplaces were once duckponds, rice paddies, and taro patches until its reefs were dredged and sand was imported to accommodate a burgeoning tourist industry in the early 1900s. Store clerks and hotel workers did not view brown kids in UH Warriors jerseys the same way they did tourists carrying Gucci handbags. The clusters of teens loitering in front of the movie theater on one side of Kalākaua looked much different—and drew much-different looks—than the tourists in linen shorts walking through the Royal Hawaiian shopping center on the other side by the beach.

As local teens, we understood these tensions, but where they stemmed from was something we barely talked about, a history we heard in passing. It was just a few blocks from here, in the late-night hours of September 12, 1931, that certain events would transpire, leading to one of the most controversial cases in Hawaiian history.

According to many at the Ala Wai Inn that September evening, Thalia Massie, a white wife of a military officer, had argued with her husband's friends and walked out alone just before midnight. When her husband, Thomas, returned home at nearly two in the morning, he called the police, saying Thalia had been assaulted by a "gang of Hawaiians." When police first questioned Thalia, she could not identify what these "Hawaiians" looked like or who they were.

It just so happened that on that same night, five Kalihi boys—Horace Ida, Benny Ahakuelo, Joseph Kahahawai, Henry Chang, and David Takai—had ditched a lūʻau in their neighborhood to go to a

92

dance at the Aloha Amusement Park in Waikīkī. On their way back home, they got into an altercation with a couple in another vehicle and sped away. Their license plate number was broadcast across police radios the next morning, including at the hospital where Thalia was being treated. By the afternoon, Thalia was at the police station, suddenly remembering the license plate number of the car her attackers were driving—and it happened to be the Kalihi boys'.

The rape trial of the five local men demonstrated the power and influence haole and the military had in Hawai'i. English-speaking papers in the islands and beyond portrayed Thalia Massie as "a woman of refinement and culture" and the young men as "fiends," whereas Japanese American papers noted that the case had caused white hysteria in the islands, with haole fearful of crime and Hawaiian gangs. These non-English papers also pointed out that had Massie not been white, she would not have been given the same benefit of the doubt or attention in Hawai'i's mainstream media. As John P. Rosa noted in his book *Local Story*, coverage of this case would also be the first time the term *local* was used to describe a group of working-class people in contrast to haole—the men were of Kanaka, Japanese, and Chinese Kanaka ancestry and had grown up about a mile away from my father's childhood home.

Thalia Massie's contradictory testimony and the police's mishandling of the case eventually led to a mistrial, but the story did not end there. Six days after the case closed, a group of navy men kidnapped and attacked Ida; less than a month after that, Massie's husband and her mother, aided by other navy men, kidnapped and killed Kahahawai. Again, mainstream papers defended the haole, describing the murder of Kahahawai as "honor killing"; high-ranking officers made comments about how "lynch laws" should prevail when the court system fails. Surprisingly, the two-week trial for the vigilantes ended in a manslaughter conviction, decided by a jury composed of half haole people and half locals. The group was sentenced to ten years of hard labor.

However, the territorial governor of Hawai'i immediately caved to pressure from the US military and government, commuting the Massies' sentence to one hour served in his office; four days later, the family sailed back to the continent forever. More than a hundred years after the first missionaries and businessmen arrived in Hawai'i, the haole elites still had the privilege to police and brutalize the locals, and now they had the protection of the US government, military, and media to get away with it.

As a young woman in Waikīkī, I'd been in hotel shops with guys and girls darker than me, in faded surf tees and slippers, who were given dirty looks and followed around by employees. Personally, though, I never felt this kind of persecution. No employees stalked my thin, light-skinned frame, even while wearing flamboyant thrift-store shirts, nor did they notice when older friends snuck me drinks at hotel pools or hideaways. I think of my father, on vacation in his board shorts, questioned by hotel workers about whether he belonged, and I can understand why he was so keen to put me in a bubble, to send me to private school, to work so hard: he didn't want me to be the kind of local that those in positions of power saw as a troublemaker, as uneducated, as poor. He believed, perhaps, I could have what he could not.

My mother and Ed could play tourist much easier; playing family was a different story.

The summer before my senior year, my mom invited me on vacation with them to Maui. I could even bring a friend, she said. I was surprised; paying for an extra person felt beyond generous for a man who wasn't supposed to know that my mom slipped me a twenty-dollar bill now and then. But I had also been on vacation with Ed before, and I remembered the regimented schedule he'd insisted on: we were up by 6:00, out the door by 6:30, eating at Denny's by 6:45 because Ed liked a menu without any surprises. Then we had to be back at the hotel by 5:00 to freshen up for dinner. It was the opposite of my dad's go-with-the-flow lounging by the pool and his showing of affection through spontaneous treats.

For this trip, I didn't bring Jen, who knew my mom and Ed best but whom I had drifted apart from, nor did I bring my closest friend, Melanie, who would have questioned how incredibly annoying Ed was. Nor did I choose my naughtiest friend, Becca, who would have found chaos in an order of Moons Over My Hammy. Instead, I brought Farrah, who had no skin in this game and was sure to please every parent and go with the flow. Farrah was also the wealthiest of my friends; her family lived in a nice modern home outside of Waikīkī, and her older sisters were off at impressive universities. Part of me hoped Farrah's respectability would force Ed to be less of an uptight cheapskate.

Ed and my mother's idea of playing tourist was not checking out the white sands of Kā'anapali Beach or the breathtaking landscapes on the road to Hāna. It was to have reasonable meals and cruise the row of shops in Lāhainā Town. For the most part, conversations remained stiff and on the surface with the buffer of Farrah around. With new company, Ed put on his jovial macho schtick, teasing Farrah about her high-pitched voice, then bursting into laughter to signal we were all to follow along and let her know that his attention was an honor. But mostly, we split off into our respective pairs, with Ed looking for a new polo shirt with "Maui" embroidered on the chest, or the two of them staying behind to have a third cup of coffee in the diner while Farrah and I ran off to the bikini store or music shop. In the afternoons, Ed went golfing, and Farrah and I were free to hang out by the pool of our '70s-era resort. We hoped to run into cute boys who also were stuck on vacation with their parents, but we came up short. Instead, we talked about all the local ska shows we'd see that summer and the party we could throw at her boyfriend's house when his parents were out of town.

The one activity the four of us all did do together was ride the Sugar Cane Train. Once used to haul sugarcane from the plantation fields in Kāʻanapali to the Pioneer Mill in Lāhainā, the steam train had been converted into a tourist ride for sightseeing, as well as rental space for weddings and kids' birthday parties. On the six-mile, slow-hummed trek, we were treated to views of the West Maui Mountains and a glimpse of the neighboring island Molokaʻi. We also got an abbreviated, skewed history lesson about Big Sugar. As the tour guide told us, settlers were gracious enough to introduce the Hawaiians to sugar production and create a booming industry for the islands. And oh, how cool was it that all the "nationalities" that came to Hawaiʻi for better lives could get along, speaking Pidgin to each other as they worked in the fields? "Ovah in Hawaiʻi, we stay one big kine melting pot," the local guide concluded with a smile. I looked over at Farrah and rolled my eyes. I was mostly annoyed that we were on a tour that seemed to be for goofy tourists and their young children, with parents chasing toddlers down the creaky, wooden aisle. The history stuff went over my head back then; it seemed to square with the shallow lessons I learned in the optional Hawaiian Studies class I took junior year. Only later would I realize how much of the picture I'd missed.

The last night we were in Maui, Ed said we'd live it up and have dinner at a cloth-napkin, sunset-view restaurant at the Sheraton. From our table by the open window, we watched families in wide-brimmed sun hats and silky cover-ups shuffle past from the pool. In the distance stood Puʻu Kekaʻa, the steep black lava rock sacred to Kānaka that's now mostly touched by tourists jumping off it into the ocean.

Opening the menu, I noticed it resembled a pricier version of Monterey Bay Canners. "Mom, can I get the crab pūpūs?" I asked. Without raising her eyes from her menu, my mom pointed out that it was a little expensive for an appetizer. I gave Farrah my "oh brother" face.

"Well, if *we* can't have pūpūs, can I order the lobster?"

This time she looked up and let out a short, stern "no."

"But I never get to have lobster," I whined about a dish I'd never even eaten before.

Ed slammed down his menu, hitting his silverware and pinging his salad fork across the table at Farrah. He pushed his seat back with the force of his body.

"What did your mother say?" He was now standing, staring down at me. I'd never seen him this upset. But I wasn't going to let him know that I was startled. I returned his stare, not saying a word.

He turned to my mother. "I told you we shouldn't have brought her."

He started heading toward the door. We had lasted all of three minutes into our nice family dinner. I turned to my mother, surprised he was actually leaving. She was shocked, too. "Jessica, look what you've done." She ran after him, putting her hand on his shoulder, whispering into his ear as he made his way toward the exit. But Ed waved his hand behind his back, shooing her away. He walked through the door and was gone.

My mom paused in the doorway, watching him before she returned to the table. I ordered the fish sandwich. The three of us didn't say a word as we finished our dinners.

An hour after we returned to our rooms that night, my mom knocked on our door and asked if she could speak to me. She guided me into the bathroom and shut the door. "You have to apologize to Ed," she said.

"For what?" I asked, reminding her that he was the one who'd said something hurtful. I asked her if it was true, if they had discussed that bringing me was a mistake. She shook her head.

Her eyes looked tired. Her hand gripped the edge of the sink. Her bony fingers always made her look older than she was. "Just do it, Jessica. It's easier that way."

When I got to their room, Ed was in the far corner, putting a pair of folded Dockers into his suitcase. I walked a few steps past the entryway and sighed. Arguing may have kept my dad around and engaged, but getting into it with Ed, I knew, would only push my mom further away.

"I'm sorry, Ed," I said, gazing at the top of his head, willing him to look up at me. He walked to the closet and began folding another pair of pants. I stood there for another second before my mom nodded. I took my cue to exit.

Back in our room, I tried to encourage Farrah to sneak out with me. Maybe we could have an adventure, hitch a ride into town, at least stroll around the hotel and just feel the potential of the night. "I don't want to get you in more trouble, Jes," she said.

I opened the sliding door to the balcony and took a seat on the chair. I stared off into the darkness, yearning for whatever else was out there. Farrah pulled up a seat next to me. We made plans for more nights at underage clubs, more afternoons at Ala Moana Beach Park, more of anything that wasn't in this moment.

Dark Spaces

I didn't have my first real, serious boyfriend until I was eighteen. His name was Isaac, and he was twenty-six.

I met him at a party during my senior year. I was interested in his friend Sam, who was tall, lanky, closer to my age, and in a local punk band called the Knumbskulls. But Sam was more interested in the party's free beer than in me. Isaac, though—short, stocky, and vaguely employed— was right there, casually joining my conversations with my friends, laughing at my jokes, and complimenting my skater shoes. He also looked at me—not my friends or any other girl who made eye contact—like I was the most beautiful girl in the room. At the end of the night, he asked me for my number, and I gave it to him.

Isaac had access to things a private school girl did not—booze, freedom, cool friends in bands like Sam. He also had a car at a time when my father had taken mine away for getting into too many fender benders. Isaac would pick my friends and me up from school and take us to play pool or sit outside of Java Java, the alt kids' coffee shop on Kapahulu. As much as I proselytized about not caring what people thought, I was still kind of embarrassed to have this older guy I wasn't necessarily attracted to roll up on campus and whisk me away. Sam, he was not.

At first, I let Isaac know I wasn't interested in him romantically, but I still tagged along with him and his friends, and he was still available to buy my friends and me wine coolers on a Saturday night. He never put a move on me, but I knew if I ever changed my mind, Isaac would jump at the chance.

Around this time, with senior year winding down, I was trying out my post–high school life. Half of my friends were preparing to go to universities on the continent. My parents had spent thousands of dollars sending me to college prep schools, and yet neither spoke to me about the college application process, taking campus tours, or my ambitions for after high school. With her finances managed by Ed, my mother mentioned once that I would need better than a B average if I wanted to score a scholarship to a school outside of Hawaiʻi. But when she told me this, I was fifteen and didn't care about a "good school" or my mother's expectations. Meanwhile, my dad didn't see the point of spending a ton of money that he didn't have when I could go to the University of Hawaiʻi and continue to live at home, like most local kids did. And I didn't push. Instead, I settled on a future at UH.

Even though I had spent much of my life dreaming of running away, I wasn't so sure I wanted to anymore. The movies depicted college life as a sequence of frat parties, stuffy ivy-clad buildings, and lots of preppy rich kids, which didn't appeal to me much. If anything, I wanted to go to a city like San Francisco or New York and be part of "a scene," but when I pictured that, I imagined experiencing life outside of a school setting. Not to mention, since I had moved out of my mother's house, I already felt less trapped. I ditched senior-year classes to go to the record store or a café with Isaac and his friends. I had my crew of girlfriends I could get into mild trouble with. We went to punk shows, where we knocked our steel-toe boots into strangers' calves. We piled into my car after dark, driving to the far end of Waikīkī, where we ran through the hotel alleyways to skinny-dip at Kaluahole Beach, feeling the chill of the water, of excitement, on our skin. My body was in constant motion, in the orbit of other bodies; I was no longer just living inside my head.

The summer after high school graduation, Isaac's and my friends would often head to the wealthy neighborhood of Kahala after sunset, carrying 40s and guitars down a tiny beach-access path that separated two plantation-style second homes that never seemed to be occupied. We sat on the beach, not too close to the estates' perimeters but far enough away for the tide to reach us. We belted the lyrics to "Here Comes Your Man" by the Pixies and "Jane Says" by Jane's Addiction and ran into the water in our underwear, the ocean stretching out before us. While Isaac may not have been the most handsome, he was the most genuine and charismatic of all his friends. Most impressive to me, he could recite the entire Talking Heads album *Stop Making Sense*, and he could do the same for Toots and the Maytals' *In the Dark* and Cecilio and Kapono's greatest hits. He had been a professional bodyboarder and was also randomly into golf and archery. For money, he could cook Italian food in a fancy restaurant, wash dishes at a mall kiosk, or build camper shells for trucks. He didn't have hang-ups about what he did for a living; he didn't have to fit one mold. He was pals with the gutter punks outside Java Java as well as the braddahs fishing off Magic Island. His family was massive. Much of his Kanaka side lived on the North Shore, and his mother was a renowned hula dancer. In other words, he was super-duper local; it felt validating that he was interested in me. But he could also traverse between scenes without any self-consciousness or having to define what he was. I was in awe.

I don't even remember the first time Isaac and I kissed, but I know, like every other kiss I'd had up until then, I was drunk. And I know I felt like if I kissed him once, I should probably kiss him the next time we hung out. Things were a little more relaxed with Isaac than they'd been with the overeager guy who waited for me outside of class. Isaac was gentler; his humor put me at ease. It was nice to touch lips, nice to do the things I saw on TV, like wrapping my arms around his neck or having my ear kissed. I remember how eager he was to go down on me in the shower of his dad's apartment when no one was home—to show me that he could offer me something that I'd want to return to.

One night, we'd had a few drinks and stumbled into his dad's apartment, where Isaac slept in the living room on a twin bed. He just hadn't bothered to clear out the second bedroom for a space of his own; it was crammed with so many T-shirts and so much old sporting gear that it was essentially a storage closet, and he slept out by the TV.

The night I lost my virginity, his father was asleep in his bedroom. Isaac went for the button on my jeans, stopping to look at me, giving me a chance to change my mind before he undid my zipper. I let him unzip me. I began tugging at his shorts button; his hand scurried over to help undo his own fly. "Should I get a condom?" he asked. I nodded and he got up, his naked body running through the love beads that separated the living room from the rest of the apartment. When he returned, I watched him put the condom on. I wasn't sure what I was supposed to do but lie there. I didn't feel much. Isaac's eyes were closed, squeezing and concentrating. Within ninety seconds, it was over.

"Isaac, what was dat?" a faraway voice called out in the dark.

"Nothing, Dad. Go back to bed," Isaac yelled, collapsing next to me. I pulled the covers over my head.

"Whatchu doing out dere?" his dad called out again. I could hear the floor creaking. His father flipped on the light switch. "Isaac! Whatchu doing?"

"Dad, go away!" he screamed. Though I couldn't see his dad's face from under the covers, I knew he could tell by my body-size lump that I was there.

"Uh, Isaac, you know bettah," he said as he went back to his bedroom. I quickly put on my clothes and drove home.

But I came back. And we had sex again and again because sex was supposed to be fun. It was supposed to be this all-fulfilling, powerful thing that was alluded to on TV and that seemed to have caused the demise of my parents' marriage. It was what I had been waiting to experience for so many years. But sex never got much more exciting than those ninety seconds, even with new positions or strange locales; for me, it was always something we were supposed to do because we were a couple.

I wasn't passionate about Isaac, but I had grown to love him. I loved that he could straddle this line of local and weirdo. I loved that my dating him irritated my mother, who thought I deserved better than a guy who never went to college and didn't have any big ambitions. She could have probably said the same for my father when they first met, and from stories, it seemed that she, too, had enjoyed frustrating her family with her romantic choice, even if she had conveniently forgotten that.

What I loved most about dating Isaac, though, was knowing that he was around. If I had a break between my college classes, I could go over to his apartment and pour a bowl of Cocoa Puffs and watch TV because there was a good chance he wasn't working. If I had a night out with friends and didn't want to drive all the way back to my dad's, I knew I could crawl into Isaac's single bed and be snuggled. I knew if I wanted company at my dad's, I could invite him over, and he'd fit right in with my brothers, playing video games with us.

For a long time, I lied to my parents and said our age difference was four years. When I came clean to Shellee, she told my dad, who confronted Isaac. "I heard you an old man fucking my daughter," my dad said, then laughed his signature deep laugh and walked away. I loved that my dad instilled fear in Isaac as much as I loved that my dad's confrontation didn't stop Isaac from loving me. We stayed together for three years. Isaac, I knew, wouldn't be the one to leave.

By my second semester at UH, I started to question why I hadn't at least looked into some cheap colleges on the continent. My friends who had come home for the holidays seemed savvier, wore lipstick, and had stories about dorm parties and guys who grew up on Martha's Vineyard, which sounded fancy. I wondered if I was missing out—or if I had ignored my out.

Then, an older student came to one of my classes to talk about studying abroad. They were promoting a semester in London. It would cost about $7,000, including plane fare, housing, most of my meals, and even some spending money. While that number was four times as much as a semester at UH, it was the equivalent of my annual tuition at Mid-Pac, which my dad had paid for years. I made the case to my parents.

My dad, I could tell, just thought this was another of my fly-by-night ideas, like wanting to take up Rollerblading or bodyboarding, both of which he had bought me equipment for that now collected dust under the house. My mom, who I thought would be supportive of me having a different cultural and educational experience, told me to ask my dad since he was the one who had the money. He was the one whose landscaping business had a good run in the '90s, after they had divorced. "I've always wanted to go to Europe, too," my mom said.

My mom had taken early retirement the year before, at the young age of fifty. Years prior, she and Ed had talked about traveling and possibly moving to Northern California. But she had come down with a variety of illnesses during my last two years of high school. First it was fibromyalgia, a disorder that caused widespread muscle pain and made her lethargic. Then it was vertigo, which brought on bouts of dizziness or spinning. Most recently, she had been diagnosed with lupus; her immune system was attacking her organs, causing her skin to blotch, her arthritis to flare up, and her lethargy to grow more extreme. Instead of traveling, she spent most of her days at home, watching TV and occasionally going to lunch at Pearlridge with me or a friend. Her retirement looked much like her home life had before, except now there was no pile of student reports to keep her busy, and she had moved her perch from the couch to her bed.

Shellee encouraged my father to let me apply to the study-abroad program, and in my sophomore year, I was off to London. Outside of a few family trips, I hadn't even seen much of the United States, and here I was about to live in another country.

On the cold January afternoon when the dozen of us students from Hawai'i arrived, the study-abroad program had arranged a tour of downtown London. We all met at the station near our school and hopped on the Tube, each of us gazing in different directions, pointing out the sexy ads or studying the map of all the color-coded train lines. When we ascended the station and were greeted by the bright lights and roundabout chaos of Piccadilly Circus, I felt an excitement in my chest like I had never known. People in smart coats skittered across the street, dodging us wide-eyed kids who were stalled in the middle of the sidewalk, both overdressed and underdressed in whatever layers we'd been able to scrounge up in Hawai'i. The neon iconography of Coca-Cola and Sanyo wrapped around the corners of buildings. Cabs and delivery trucks zoomed out from every nook of the five-way intersection. Among all the modern flash towered ornate Edwardian-era monstrosities adorned with domes, arches, and pillars. A bronze fountain at the center of it all tied the whole scene together. I loved the sensory overload. I knew right then and there I was a city girl.

But over the next week, I had a harder time enjoying all the new experiences I was thrust into—trips to the theater, the National Gallery, Buckingham Palace. My mind started to race. I missed Isaac; I missed my chicken katsu plate lunch; I missed my three hundred channels of crappy American television. I could not ground my mind in the present.

I called my mom several times a day with new ideas for how I could fix my uneasiness. Maybe I could use my spending money to fly Isaac over here, I suggested. I could give up my shared room in my homestay, and he and I could rent a flat together. That way, I wouldn't be giving up, just moving my life in London closer to normal, I told her. When my plans hit a roadblock—Isaac was disinterested in uprooting his life—I called my mother, threatening to come home. Nothing I did would quell my anxiety.

My mother called the head of the exchange program at the university. "Being away from the islands can be a big adjustment for a local kid," the coordinator at UH told her. "They are used to having 'ohana around and orienting themselves with the knowledge that the mountains and ocean are always on either side. Being in a big city, with people not making eye contact, focused on their own stuff, can take getting used to," the coordinator said.

But as the days went on, I didn't get used to it. I couldn't find a way to feel more at ease. And though we never addressed it, my mom surely remembered the oversensitive kid who had cried "fire" in the movie theater.

After nothing else worked, my mom put in a call to my dad. As much as my dad was the one who fixed things, I had avoided calling him because he hated hysterics. ("Crying doesn't work on me," he'd once yelled, which had only made me cry more.) And I knew if I had talked to Shellee, she would have just reported everything to him.

True to form, when my dad finally called, he did not hesitate to force some perspective. "Do you know what I was doing wen I was your age, Jessica? Do you have any idea? I wasn't on my parents' dime prancing around Europe. My ass was being dragged to Vietnam. I fought in a war. A war, Jessica. Do you think I wanted to go dere? Do you think I had fun? Am I supposed to feel sorry for you because you have it rough in England?"

His words were almost logical enough to shake some sense into me. But as much as I knew I was acting ridiculous, as much as I wanted to chill out, I felt like I had no control over my brain. As I sat in my homestay's hallway, cradling the communal phone, my face was wet with snot and tears.

"But, Dad, I feel so alone," I told him.

"Alone? Let me let you in on a secret, Jessica: all you have in life is yourself."

His words stung. They felt scary, and they felt anti-'ohana, but they also felt true. I'd remember them again and again.

For the next few days, I stopped myself from picking up the phone when my mind started hopscotching through worries. My neighbors across the hall, students from Michigan, no doubt had picked up that I was depressed and asked one night if I wanted to go to a club with them. I threw on my coat.

The place ended up being less like a stylish European disco and more like a glorified sports bar. The TVs mounted on the walls played soccer highlights, and in the middle of the room was a dropped dance floor. Brit-pop and sappy American hits blared from loudspeakers, but most of the crowd—pale, boisterous guys—were fixated on the muted TV screens. It was not a club I would've chosen, but at that point, I was barely making choices. The noise, the elbows brushing past me, the movement of my hand to my mouth were enough to keep me busy.

Unable to hear what anyone was saying, my housemates and I just kept passing our pints around our little group to sample. We sipped chocolate stouts, chugged ciders. After about three or four beers, we were all on the dance floor, singing along to that horribly catchy Chumbawamba tune, a song I'd hated on the radio at home but rang in my ears in glory. "I get knocked out, but I get up again. You're never gonna keep me down." Bodies were jammed all around me; the strobe light caught my face. I swayed my arms over my head, closed my eyes, and realized, right then and there, I felt pretty damn good. My anxiety, for the moment, had disappeared.

While I drank every now and then before I'd left for London, I formed a steady habit of partying while I was there. I danced at the Limelight, where we smashed into guys during the Prodigy's punchy "Firestarter" and American rock staples like Nirvana's "Smells Like Teen Spirit." I saw bands I loved, like Erasure, the Misfits, and the Toasters. Some nights ended with exchanged numbers and jokes made on street corners; others with drunk-buying postcards and mock-singing Spice Girls songs on my slog home.

You never knew what you were going to get when you set out with a to-go cup of cider and jumped on the Tube—and that anticipation was the greatest high. It was just like the '80s hair-metal videos had promised.

The semester passed in a blur, and back in Hawai'i, I didn't settle back down. I went out to "clubs" on school nights; restaurants turned into after-hours hot spots with bands and DJs. While each genre had its own small scene—goths, punks, metalheads, hip-hop heads, house heads, rude boys, the reggae bunch—there was a lot of overlap. Partially because blending is the credo in Hawai'i and partially because in a city of under a million people, there were only so many cool things to do on a given night. Being part of "the scene" in Hawai'i did not mean spending big bucks and going to flashy clubs (those didn't really exist); it meant being able to "talk story" with the crew of people who were always out and about. It meant jumping the line at Indigo's because you knew the promoter who happened to be chatting up a friend of yours as you walked by. Or becoming pals with the bartender at Nick's Fishmarket and doing a shot or three with him right before closing time. Or being invited to the impromptu freestyle sessions at some guy's Chinatown apartment. And it often meant ending up at the Wave, a basic club at the edge of Waikīkī, because it was one of the few places open till 4:00, and the last thing you wanted to do was go home.

In these spaces, in these conversations where we had to scream over the speakers, I felt part of something. "Hey, have you met Jessica?" one friend asked another, all three of us bellied up to the bar. We exchanged local-style kisses, one on each cheek, greeting each other with our contagious aloha smiles. I skanked, stomped, and moshed to bands whose members I became buddies with after the show. Girls invited me into their conversations, and guys looked at me with slight interest but mostly saw me as one of them. We did shots, acted like pirates, sang the theme to *Golden Girls* seven drinks deep on the sidewalk after the bar's lights came on. With kamikazes and Guinnesses rolling through my body, I didn't worry about what I'd say next. I could get close to people, lean into their shoulders, laugh in their ears, the kind of laugh that shakes the room. I felt a kind of safety in being wanted and included.

My favorite scene was goth-lite. There, I could just dance to '80s post-punk and darkwave like Book of Love, New Order, and Sisters of Mercy. These spaces were quieter, cozier than the gregarious crowds of other scenes. Little cliques in corners sipped their double-well-drink specials and danced to their favorite songs, which were all of them. I landed a job as a door girl, a dream side gig that gave me forty dollars cash, an open bar tab, and the opportunity to dance while keeping an eye on who was coming in.

Unlike in the other scenes that I was part of, socializing came second or even third to the music and the dancing. Everyone was a regular; everyone wanted that release. The music was so moody, so raw, the room so literally dark and full of brown people in black clothes who, maybe, like me, needed an outlet for their sadness or anxiety or discontent. And yet there was so much joy on that dance floor. A few dozen people, arms flailing, spin-waltzing, going all the way off to the tempo-shifting howls of Siouxsie Sioux. I never felt more at home, my mind and body more free, than on that dance floor. For those four hours every Thursday, that tiny bar over a laundromat in Waikīkī was a space for local weirdos to be together, alone.

If high school had been a maze of labels that felt exhausting to navigate, college was a path I could create and conquer, filling nearly every hour of every day. I loved sociology, my major, and going deep on things we only scratched the surface of in everyday conversations, like race and drugs and nature versus nurture. I tacked on a double major in journalism, thinking I could write about these issues—or what I *really* wanted to write about: music. I got nearly straight As while working twenty to thirty hours a week at internet coffee shops and a family chain restaurant, where, after every shift, I immediately spent all my tip money at the bars downtown with my coworkers. I answered phones at the suicide and crisis hotline on Sundays and landed an internship at the *Honolulu Weekly* several afternoons a week, reporting on local goings-on and eventually scoring a nightlife column. I even promoted my own '80s darkwave night at a gay club.

In the evenings when there was not much else happening, I hung out with my boyfriend—first Isaac, then a gothy local guy who was studying IT at UH and was also kind and steady. Even if I stayed out all hours and parked my car crooked in the driveway just before sunrise, my dad and Shellee didn't say much because I made good grades, kept a job, and was working toward my ambitions. It felt like I had it together, bolstered by the safety of my rent-free bubble.

But in all that juggling, there was one task I felt compelled to do without being asked: spending half a day once a week with my mother.

By my senior year in college, my mom was getting sicker, more sedentary. Most days, she was confined to her bed. Her lupus had advanced, and her mobility was made worse when she broke her hip during a fall in the grocery store. Then she hurt her back when she fell getting out of bed in the middle of the night. Her growing list of ailments now included sciatica, and she had to use a walker most days. She hoped it would be temporary. Our trips to meet halfway at Pearlridge were off the table; it was easier if I met her at her and Ed's house, now a smaller townhouse in Makakilo.

On these days, I would arrive to find Ed in the living room, watching football or an old Western. We'd mumble "hi" to each other as I walked straight into their bedroom.

Over a decade into their marriage, some of their rosy togetherness had faded. My mom no longer pretended to care about exercise or golf (Ed could do that on his own time), and she was too ill to sit comfortably through church (he could do that by himself, too). She'd rather watch her soaps and leave Ed to his own programming. The three of us had also long since stopped trying or pretending to do things together, including dinner—short hellos and the occasional "What are you watching?" were about as complex as my relationship got with Ed.

In my mother's bedroom, she would already have that week's *People* and *Entertainment Weekly* magazines laid out for me on my side of the bed. "How far behind are you on *General Hospital?*" she'd ask. Even if she watched the episodes in real time, she still taped them so that we could watch together.

It was the era of big, juicy storylines we loved—Sonny, the hot gangster, and his forbidden love, the even hotter Brenda; Robin, who was my age, and her sweet boyfriend, Stone, who had AIDS. We talked about Brenda's perfect hair; we cried when Robin got an HIV diagnosis. Sometimes I'd tell my mom about my goth boyfriend, and I could tell she didn't think he was suitable for me. He came from a broken family (like me) and lived in public housing with his grandma. Sometimes I gave her my latest *Honolulu Weekly* column, and when I came back the next week, it would still be on her dresser, untouched. "Oh, I'm sorry. I forgot," she would say when I asked. I didn't understand what else was occupying her time. It didn't dawn on me how hard it might have been for her to see that I was growing up without her.

Instead, she led the conversation topics, often ones without consequence. "I swear to god, the mail lady steals my magazines," she said when one of her latest issues failed to show up.

"Mom, of all the mail she delivers, why would she steal magazines? And why yours?" I asked.

"I don't know, but she does. Sometimes, they even look like they've been flipped through."

I shook my head. "Whatever, Mom."

But I wasn't necessarily looking for anything deeper. It was nice to check out and spend a few hours at my mom's townhome, flipping through gossip rags and staring at the television, after a heavy schedule of studying, working, and partying. All that was expected of me was to lie there, maybe giggle at her jokes and rub her arm. That I could do, without thinking about what all these accumulating illnesses and ailments actually meant.

Around 6:00, she asked me to grab money out of her purse and buy all three of us dinner. More than fifteen years after it was promised, the second city of Kapolei had finally risen in a cluster of strip malls that offered a number of fast-food joints and supermarket chains below Makakilo. My mom often opted for Jack in the Box, and Ed would eat his healthy chicken breast sandwich in the living room while my mother and I ate our greasy fried ones in bed from our lap trays, the same ones we'd used all those years ago in the dropped living room.

I liked to go over on Thursdays and watch the prime-time lineup of *Friends* and *Seinfeld*. But once *Will & Grace* came on, I had to go because it was time to head to the darkwave night I was running. My mom always asked if I could just stay through the first commercial, and sometimes I did, before changing into a sluttier top and long, flowy skirt and walking out the door and into the night that lay ahead of me.

The spring before my college graduation in 2000, my mother had her worst bout with lupus yet. Her lungs filled up with fluid, and her white blood cells attacked her organs. Her team of doctors—a rheumatologist (lupus), a nephrologist (kidneys), and a general physician—admitted her to the hospital, and for two weeks, they pumped her up with hormones and steroids to drain the fluid, only for the white blood cells to continue to multiply.

One afternoon when I walked into her hospital room, she told me the next step was chemotherapy.

"Chemotherapy?" I asked, coming around to her on the bed. "But you don't have cancer."

She shrugged, telling me it was supposed to be in the pill form.

My mother was always very accepting of whatever her doctors said. She didn't prod further once test results came in, and she wasn't one to try a change in diet or exercise or even acupuncture, like my friends' parents, who came from Eastern backgrounds, had suggested. Meanwhile, I questioned all authority. "There are things I need to ask this doctor," I declared, even though I had never taken any opportunity to ask my mom for clarity about her health before.

The next day, when one of the doctors peeked in to see how my mother was doing, I hammered him with questions: How will the chemo affect her? Will she lose her hair? How long will she have to be on it?

"If this doesn't work, then what?" I asked him.

"She's a budding journalist," my mother interrupted, smiling at the doctor. I shot her a "shut up" glance.

"Well, we'll reassess," he answered. "We're doing our best." With that, he nodded and walked out of the room.

Later that afternoon, Ed stopped by while my mom was taking a nap. He took the chair on the other side of her bed, opposite me. We sat there for a few minutes in silence, glaring at the news on the mounted television in the corner. There was construction going on at the airport. The surf report forecasted three to five feet on the east side for the following day.

I leaned across her sleeping body. "Do you think she's going to be OK?" I whispered to him.

"She's tough," he said. "She'll pull through." *Tough* wasn't a word I associated with my mother. But I wanted to believe him. His confidence let me think that he would be the one to take care of her so that I wouldn't have to.

Kuleana is one's personal sense of responsibility—responsibility to the 'āina, to the community, to your 'ohana. It is a guiding principle of the Kānaka. It runs through your work, your care, your everyday to-and-fro.

My father's kuleana as a landscaper, for example, was to plant native trees that nourished the soil and install irrigation systems that were conscientious of water conservation. My mother's kuleana, you could say, was making her students feel heard and inspired, even if she was teaching American literature instead of Hawaiian mo'olelo.

My sense of kuleana had always felt very American. Duty, to me, meant to achieve, to avoid disappointment, to build something others would be proud of. Even as a writer, I didn't see my local nightlife column serving a greater purpose of community, although, in a weird way, it did; my goal was to impress readers, to make them think, "Wow, what a cool gig she has!" or "Solid point!"

Caring for what was already before me, and conveying that care, was not so much what I prioritized in the day-to-day. It's not that I went out of my way to disregard the land or my mother. But I didn't want to come to terms with how much care she actually needed. I didn't want to tell her how much her fragility scared me. I couldn't imagine life without her. And ever the image of composure, she didn't discuss her fears and futures with me, either.

Once she was out of the hospital, we went back to our weekly visits in bed, watching soaps and filling up on fast food, even though she was clearly more dependent, her health more fragile. I didn't feel empowered, or even purposeful, as I helped her to her walker just so that she could scuttle to the bathroom, nor did I feel helpful in fetching her Hershey's Miniatures when she had a craving every handful of minutes. It felt sad, a reminder that all these hours in bed weren't downtime—this was her life, and the little variety she had was to pee and enjoy some candy. I wouldn't allow myself to think where this path ended, where the depths of kuleana and ties to my 'ohana might take me. My instinct was to get out while I could.

That June when I graduated from college, I applied for several editorial internships—three that were far away in New York City and one that was in LA. I assumed I was past falling into the homesickness-anxiety pits like I did in London. I told friends that I wanted a challenge, career opportunities bigger than the local paper. I didn't say anything about not wanting to watch my mother die.

Los Angeles Magazine got back to me first. My mother's lupus was in remission. She was back to blithely chatting about Brenda falling for the wrong man on *General Hospital*. I told my editor I could be there in two weeks.

Pele ran from home, too. But her circumstances were a bit different from mine.

In common moʻolelo, Pele was born to Earth Mother Papa and Sky Father Wākea on Kahiki, better known as Tahiti. Her ʻohana was extensive. She had a brother who was a shark, a sister who could make snow, and many more siblings whom she loved deeply and sparred with intensely. But before her youngest sister, Hiʻiaka, was even part of this world, it was Pele's relationship with her older sister Nāmakaokahaʻi, the goddess of the sea, that had a far-reaching impact.

Pele knew she was different at a young age. While the rest of her siblings splashed in the ocean, rolling with the tides, Pele stayed on land. Her uncle Lonomakua, the keeper of flame, sensed Pele's special powers, taking her under his wing and sharing his knowledge. He taught her about the layers of soil and rock. He brought her to a darkened cave and gave her an ʻōʻō, or digging stick, to practice striking the earth and building flames. When she succeeded, her blaze filling the cave with light, its heat swelling to shake the ʻāina, it was clear that commanding fire was Pele's kuleana.

Even though Nāmaka had powers of her own, she was jealous of Pele's potential. She was also sure that Pele and her uncle were the ones causing the hot spots under the sea and warned her family that they'd get burned if Pele kept this up. In one telling, Pele taps her ʻōʻō, accidentally causing a quake that sends a chunk of ʻāina into the ocean, destroying Nāmaka's home. Furious, Nāmaka warns that a tsunami is coming—if she can't have a home, then Pele won't have one, either.

With all this tension disrupting the family, Pele decides to take off. She will find a place where she can harness her powers. As a parting gift, Pele's mother gives her an egg; she is to keep it warm, care for it. Inside resides Hiʻiaka.

Pele sets sail in a canoe, her siblings swimming beside her, guiding the way with their knowledge of the sea. First, they come across the island of Niʻihau. When Pele steps out of the canoe, she notices that the ʻāina is too damp to hold her fire and moves on. She continues east, landing on Kauaʻi. Pele digs a crater with her ʻōʻō to hold her flame, but Nāmaka rolls in as another tsunami, putting out her fire. Pele flees once more.

She tries Oʻahu, then Molokaʻi, then Lānaʻi, but Nāmaka appears again and again, extinguishing every blaze Pele creates. By the time Pele arrives on Maui and sees Nāmaka right behind her, she decides to stop running. The sisters go flame to wave until it appears Pele has perished. Nāmaka has won. She returns to the sea, alone, having successfully pushed her ʻohana away.

Little does she know, however, that her siblings helped create a passageway for Pele to escape to Kīlauea on the Big Island. (Some moʻolelo, though, say Pele did die, and it is her spirit that resides in the volcano.) It is here that Pele reaches her full potential, making her home in the Halemaʻumaʻu Crater, bursting forth rivers of fire, her steam wafting through the forests of Puna. With the nurturing of her sister, Hiʻiaka is the first of the Pele ʻohana born in Hawaiʻi.

There are a number of lessons to derive from this moʻolelo. For instance, my idea that the quintessential ʻohana resides in perpetual harmony is unrealistic and absurd—a number of Pele 'ohana stories are laced with mana wahine and support, but there are also tales of the siblings' epic battles; families are, indeed, complicated. Like most mo'olelo, Pele's search for a home is also a clear example of the power and symbiosis of nature, how the elements are stronger than the will of any god or mortal.

It would be easy for me to side with Pele, an outsider willing to risk what was familiar to take a chance on a home more fitting. But I can't help but feel for Nāmaka, alone, angry, unwilling to bridge the rift of disconnection. She loved her family, and yet she chose isolation. This weight, I can only imagine, made it impossible to ever get comfortable, even if she gave herself purpose and distracted herself with trouble.

PART TWO

Mai hōʻeuʻeu mai ʻoe
I ka wai ua lana mālie
E kakali mālie ʻoe
A laʻi pono ka makani

You must not be anxious to rush
Into the water that appears serene
You must wait patiently
Until the wind calms down

—"Mai Hōʻeuʻeu Mai ʻOe," traditional
Hawaiian mele

The Nag in My Naʻau

I was in LA all of three months before I ended up in jail.

The night started off at our apartment, a two-bedroom I shared with an acquaintance in North Hollywood—not to be confused with the television glamour of Hollywood or even the quirky antiseptics of the current NoHo. Our North Hollywood, the North Hollywood at the turn of the millennium, was a corridor of used-car joints, tire stores, and furniture depots that touted "blowout" sales with no end date. It was a Wienerschnitzel on one corner and a sex shop on the other. The pool in our apartment complex was filled with concrete.

I had just finished a day of fact-checking arts pieces at my nonpaying internship. My roommate, Mong, whom I knew from Hawaiʻi, had just wrapped up a shift at a car-rental place, one of the three jobs she held to save money to buy her own vehicle. We had been waiting for this moment since our alarms blasted us into the day—the sun down, the promise of night ahead of us. Except our promise was on a budget, so we grabbed our jugs of Relska vodka and cranberry juice and downed a few drinks to get a head start. Then it was into my car, over the hill into West Hollywood, and down Sunset Boulevard. Tonight was the night that we would make the pilgrimage to the Rainbow Bar and Grill.

The Rainbow was the stuff of hair-metal lore. It's where Guns N' Roses partied in the "November Rain" video and where Lemmy from Motörhead still bellied up to the bar after hitting up the strip club next door. Our quest was based on earnest nostalgia—we knew it was goofy to go there, but as two young women who had devoured the all-fun-no-consequences antics of these bands growing up, we also knew we were guaranteed to get into some mischief.

At the door, we paid the ten-dollar cover in exchange for two drink tickets, which we maximized by ordering Long Beaches, a mix of five well liquors with a splash of cran. Inside, the bar was dark and damp like a basement, the low ceiling strung with Christmas lights and weighed down by secrets. The red booths in the back were occupied by rocker types in leather hats, eating pizza and holding court. Older men, including Lemmy himself, sat at the bar, engrossed in whatever drink or human was at arm's length. With nowhere to sit, Mong and I huddled in the center of the room, screaming over the Danzig that blared out of the speakers, which felt awkward, so we went upstairs, past the second-floor bathrooms, to the attic. The idea was to keep moving—to not think about how much we thought about where we belonged.

Up on the third floor, the bass line of a System of a Down song rattled the walls. Mong and I didn't hesitate to hit the dance floor. There was plenty of space to flail our arms, thrash our heads, and stomp. We weren't the type of girls who danced seductively with one another, one shimmying down to the other's cleavage or grinding from behind. We were usually too drunk to put that much effort into our moves. I enjoyed the unconsciousness. Our bodies and minds unattached to a single motive, absorbing the music, free to do as they pleased.

However, if our dance-floor antics garnered us any attention, we weren't dumb enough to turn it away.

The only two guys on the dance floor who were our age were cute enough, long and lanky, each with a mess of curly hair. I have no idea what we said to them (probably that we were from Hawai'i) or they to us (I'm pretty sure they told us they grew up in the LA neighborhood of Little Armenia), but by the time the lights came up, we had agreed to go with them next door to an after-hours club.

But wait, I had to pull my car out of the lot first, I told them. It closed at 2:00 a.m., and I didn't want it to get locked in.

We all jumped into my Explorer and I threw it in reverse. Then—bam!—I hit the car behind me. My instinct was not to check out the damage or even pause. It was to put my car in drive and speed toward the exit.

The parking attendant had a different idea. "Where do you think you're going?" he screamed, catching up to my car as I tried to pull out onto Sunset Boulevard. I rolled down my window and looked into his eyes—he was around my age—and pleaded for him to let me go.

He looked at me like I was bonkers. No, he told me. A line of cars had formed behind me to get out of the lot. A cacophony of horns beeped. "Please," I said, trying one last time.

But the attendant was not going to risk his livelihood for an incoherent woman with smeared burgundy lipstick. "Park across the street and come back. I have your plate number," he told me.

By the time I had found a spot and the four of us walked back to the lot, the cops were there waiting for us. Our new hesher friends, to their credit, did not take off running. I crookedly walked lines and chanted to myself to think sober thoughts. When the officer asked me to follow his flashlight, I did so with my entire floppy head instead of just my pupils. Mong, meanwhile, asked if she could go puke. She walked all of five feet before vomiting on the sidewalk. The next thing I knew, I had my hands behind my back and I was sitting in the cop car. From the back seat window, I watched the iconic lights of the Roxy, the Whiskey a Go Go, and the Viper Room zoom by. A twinge of giddiness hit me. Finally, *something* was happening.

About twenty minutes later, I was crying as the cop fingerprinted me. I was still crying as I made my one phone call to our apartment and blathered who knows what into the answering machine when Mong didn't answer. What I can recall is that four hours later, I woke up in a panic, alone on a concrete bench in a gray cell with a steel door. There were no bars to shake, no other misfit women to commiserate with like there are in the movies. For about ten minutes, I jumped up and down in front of the door's peephole, trying to get anyone's attention. Thirty minutes later, a guard dropped off a tray of gray eggs. "Maybe this afternoon, maybe Monday," she said when I asked her about getting out. By the end of the hour, I was kneeling in front of the seatless toilet with my finger down my throat. Nothing came out.

Hula is about feeling. And where you feel it is behind the piko, or belly button, in the na'au. It's a warmth from your gut, connecting you to what's come before and what's around you now—the breeze at your back, the fallen plumeria on the ground—expressed through the hands, the weight of your body shifting from the ball of your foot to your toes.

Hula is a recentering, because moments of disconnection and pain exist. If you can recognize when things are not quite right, then what you need to reground yourself is right there—your surroundings, your ancestors, your own body. That twist of the hand, that focus on how Hi'iaka created pali 'a'ala, or fragrant cliffs, in the wake of Pele's fire, is an intention to find rebirth in destruction, to release the suffering. Hula is not a dance for the unconscious and unattached.

When the missionaries arrived in Hawai'i and saw both women and men with their chests bare, their hips moving in rhythm with the ocean, they saw something sexual. An energy that stirred up feelings they had learned were uncomfortable, even sinful. They had no understanding that the Kānaka were interpreting the wind, the darkness of the mountain, the sharing of tears, and yes, sex. It did not matter that their dances were stories that had been passed down through generations, a way to keep their ancestors and healing alive. Hula had woken an unease in the missionaries, so it was to be banned.

Today, the hula lives again in schools and hālau both inside and outside of Hawai'i, a way for Kānaka, locals, and others to reconnect to their heritage, nature, and themselves. I took hula for a few months in preschool before switching to ballet, my mom trying to do the things parents of Hawaiian children should do before reverting to what was familiar. But I remember watching hula performances at my high school for May Day. Otherwise known as "lei day in Hawai'i nei," the holiday was created in 1927 by a poet and ad writer originally from Oklahoma to honor lei giving; today, most schools in Hawai'i recognize the day with a hula program and the crowning of a king and queen to the May Day court. Watching these performances, I was mesmerized by the grace and sway of the dancers in one song, then the strength and centering beat of the ipu hitting the ground in the next. I could see the stories they were telling, from the picking of pīkake flowers to the heat of the sun, even if I didn't understand the words of the mele. But what moved me most was the way some dancers just seemed to get it, beyond practice and dedication. Sacred chants and basic footwork can be taught through focus and repetition, but I imagine the hardest part is learning how to harness that energy in your na'au.

How does one relearn that connection after being told for generations to sever it? Because the more I felt a stirring in my na'au, the more my impulse was to numb it.

Hangovers are terrible not just because they are physically excruciating—the headaches, nausea, and discomfort caused by dehydration; the immune system scrambling to keep up—but because they are mentally torturous as well. Between half naps and dry heaves, there's the ping-pong of piecing together last night's cringey moments with the guilt of whatever was said and done in those spaces. As I lay in my own bed the evening I was released from jail, worrying about my impending fines and unknown consequences, I wanted to unburden myself, if not physically, then mentally. I knew I could never tell my mom I got a DUI because—I believed, at that point—she'd never fucked up anything in her life. So I dialed my dad.

Unlike the aftermath of the many fender benders I'd gotten into as a teenager, my dad didn't yell at me. He told me how he'd been arrested for a DUI, too, when he was my age. He was on his motorcycle and thought he was so smart, so akamai, he could outrun the cops. In the end, he could not. Still, he told me to fight the charge since the cops didn't technically see me driving. "You'll get chroo it," he said.

Just months earlier, my dad had helped me settle into LA. He had never lived off-island, outside of being drafted to Vietnam; moving away, he knew, was a big deal for a local girl. He said I should ship my car because it was cheaper than buying something in California and helped me narrow down neighborhoods that fit my tight budget. He even cosigned my lease since I had no credit. He was there to set me up, then let me go.

But in between logistics like getting a cashier's check and buying a towel rack from the dollar store, my father paid for sushi lunches and for us to get away from North Hollywood to watch bands we found in the local alt-weekly. We saw a Latin rock–hip-hop band, something we wouldn't find in Hawai'i, and went to the House of Blues on an off night, hoping to run into some lesser-known virtuoso. Away from work and obligations, my father was up for whatever I was into, even if it was just the comfort of pancakes and hot chocolate in a tacky diner. He was giving me one last hurrah before I segued into my own scrappy adult life.

One night while we were having dinner, I thought about my mother, holed up alone in her bed. "Do you think this was a good idea, my moving away?" I asked him without mentioning my mother.

My dad looked up from his plate. "I don't worry about you," he said. "I only worry because you're fearless."

He surely meant I was mouthy and did dumb things like getting behind the wheel after seven drinks. But I took it as a compliment. The bravest guy I knew thought I was just like him. I had to prove him right.

Since the magazine internship did not pay, I hoped to wait tables until the music journalism job of my dreams fell into my lap. After being asked for résumés and headshots and to come back for auditions, it became clear that I could not compete with the early-aughts LA women hired at the hippest restaurants and bars, the type who had been in the city long enough to earn some money and spent it on looking the part: professionally done chunky blonde highlights; a shade-three tan; impeccably penciled-in eyebrows; a rock vibe with low-rise designer jeans, a studded belt, and a tight ribbed undershirt. If you did not look like a cross between a Playboy Bunny and circa-2000 Gwen Stefani, no need to apply.

Since I did not, I ended up packing to-go orders at an Italian restaurant in the Valley. Some of my roles involved hostessing in my unsexy uniform of an oversize navy button-down and polyester black slacks, but most of my time was spent in the kitchen with the boys—the Brazilian delivery guys, the Guatemalan and Salvadoran line cooks, and the hot busser Carlos—where every interaction felt mildly flirtatious. Sexual tension extended throughout the restaurant—just like at any restaurant, really, where young people work. Gay, straight, single, married, no one was off-limits for a dirty innuendo or even a too-close whisper. But there was definitely a division between the mostly white waitstaff and bartenders in the front of the house and the brown, mostly male staff in the back. There always is.

In the back, there was a lot of silly banter, as well as attempts to teach me relevant Spanish words (pendeja, guapa, ochenta y seis pepperoni). But we also chatted about where we were from. They told me about their moms and sisters and families back home; how being here was just for now, to make money, to return. When they asked me about Hawai'i, I told them that it was nice but that I had gotten bored. There was so much of the world I wanted to see. "Maybe we could all go to the dive across the street one night or to watch a band in Hollywood?" I suggested. They looked at me like I was bonkers. They had to save money; they had to get up early. "I don't go over the hill too much," Jorge, the sous chef, told me. A few times after a day shift, several of us went to a nearby pupusería where we shared queso pupusas and carne asada and drank Tecates from cans. There was a casualness, an openness between us that reminded me of back home. While people in LA were mostly nice, I also felt like I had to look a certain way for people to *really* be nice to me. Except when I was standing around in the kitchen, bullshitting and snacking on leftover pizza.

But the minute I left the restaurant every night, a burst of anxiety swept through me. The last place I wanted to go was back to my apartment. I got into my car in the back alley, turned the key in the ignition, and thought about what dark, loud room I could escape to and which of my few friends I could convince to meet me anywhere I was willing to go. After all those years, I still hated the quiet of home.

With the status of my license in limbo, Mong and I tried to fulfill our night promises closer to our apartment, at least for a while. This was years before Uber or Lyft existed, when we only knew of people taking cabs to the airport. Not that we would have ponied up for a ride anyway. Instead, we drove a mile to the local dive, where we'd sometimes see character actors from childhood sitcoms. It was there I met Robbie.

I caught Robbie staring at us, smiling, as Mong and I swayed to the Cure's "Just Like Heaven" playing on the jukebox. He had a handsome, boyish face and gelled black hair that made him look a little like the Count from *Sesame Street*. I walked over.

"I saw you looking at me," I told him. He admitted he was. Even though he was dressed in head-to-toe black, Robbie was all smiles, with a chipper squeakiness to his voice as we chatted about music. I could tell he thought I was out of his league, even though I wasn't. I gave him my number.

Robbie was a second-generation Mexican American who worked at a record store but could somehow afford a perpetually sparkly Jetta and shiny leather wing tips (likely because he still lived with his parents in Northridge). My work crew, although they'd barely met him, did not like Robbie—he was a try-too-hard, they thought. To be honest, I wasn't sold on Robbie, either. The squeak in his voice never stopped being alarming; he was an even sunnier goth than I was. But he loved to take me to places I hadn't been to yet, and he picked me up and paid for it all. He was also always down for another drink. We emptied Jägerbombs after vodka tonics after bottles of Negra Modelo on a random Wednesday before 7:00 p.m. Like me, he didn't fit in with his childhood surroundings—his parents were from Mexico, but he barely spoke Spanish, nor did he participate in much Mexican tradition aside from eating his mother's cooking—and he was a black sheep in high school, not for being bad but for dressing dark, like from a coffin. Our greatest bond was music and what it invoked within us. We blasted Placebo in his Jetta as we flew down Sepulveda after midnight, both of us high on cheap liquor and the possibility of what lay ahead, which was usually half fooling around, half passing out drunk. But Robbie also listened to my stories of how I promoted my own '80s night and got into shows for free as a local reporter. He made me feel likable, interesting, accomplished, not the girl who had few friends and a job wrapping lasagna.

One night, when we were at a bar in West Hollywood, Robbie moved in close to me and whispered in my ear, "Am I your boyfriend?"

I kept looking straight ahead at the green beer bottles lining the back of the bar. "I don't like labels," I told him, a line I'd probably heard in a movie the day before.

He thumbed the rim of his beer, his head down.

I could have excused myself to the bathroom, broken the awkward silence with talk of the new CD I'd just bought, but I just sat there, jiggling my empty drink, sucking on the cubes, lingering in his discomfort.

A few hangouts later, a group of us had been out drinking and wound up back at my apartment. My friends cracked open more beers and talked about going to an after-party. Robbie grabbed my hand and gave me a look that said he was done for the night. I wasn't. "I think I'm too drunk," he said. "I wanna go to bed." I didn't want to cause a scene in front of my friends, so I turned his body toward the stairs and followed him up to my bedroom before anyone else could notice we had bailed.

Up in my room, the door closed, and he pulled me toward him for a kiss. I pulled away. "I thought you were tired," I said.

"Not too tired for some of this"—he nibbled into my ear, pulling me back in—"or some of this," he said, grabbing the small of my back.

I released myself from him again. "Yeah, well, I actually want to check out that other party," I said.

Tears welled in his eyes. "But, Jessica, I love you," he said. The words tumbled out of his mouth so effortlessly.

I stood there, watching him like he was on a television screen. I left him in my bed and walked out the door. I went to the party.

In the spring of 2001, about six months after my arrest, I was finally sentenced for my DUI. Unlike what my dad had hoped, I could not fight it. Instead, I got $1,000 in fines, three years of probation, six weeks of mandatory alcohol education classes, and twenty AA meetings. If I violated my probation with another DUI, I would have to do jail time without question.

With many of my days free, I attended midday AA meetings a few blocks from my apartment in an abandoned storefront in a tucked-away strip mall. I could have driven over the hill to attend meetings sprinkled with celebrities at wellness centers, but I wasn't looking to make the experience fun or useful. I just wanted to get it over with.

I always arrived at AA with a scowl and in a mad dash to take a seat in the far back corner. I slouched in my chair, arms crossed. I never spoke. As I looked around the room at the dozen or so middle-aged white men drinking watery coffee, I told myself I did not belong there. I did not need to make conversation before or after a meeting, and I didn't need to recite AA jargon. "It works because I worked it," one said. "The answers to my problems came because my house was in order," said another. I didn't see these AA members as people brave enough to reach for a lifeline. Maybe because I didn't want to see myself as some-one who needed one, too. What I did do was make sure everyone saw me wave my court order in the group leader's face for a signature at the end of each meeting.

In the alcohol education classes, though, I was forced to participate. Here, all of us were court ordered, most of us hadn't surrendered to a higher power, and many of us could think of better ways to spend a Sunday morning. For several hours every week, we watched videos and did group activities after being lectured on the dangers of drunk driving. It was a lesson in humility, whether we wanted it or not.

During one of our last classes, the instructor walked around, asking the dozen of us how we had changed, or planned to change, any of our drinking habits. One man said he was going to work on repairing his relationship with his wife; another was going to apply for an office job at the old company where he used to be a driver. While my classmates didn't seem as foreign to me as my AA contingent, they still seemed a lot worse off than I was. Most were older and had complicated family issues because of what I deemed "legitimate" drinking problems. I convinced myself that I was just a single twenty-three-year-old acting like a single twenty-three-year-old, and unfortunately for me, I was just one of the few who got caught doing what most twenty-three-year-olds do.

By the time it was my turn to answer, everyone in the room had at least said they were trying to curb their drinking. I said that I'd stopped driving when I drank—and even that wasn't completely true. I had stopped pacing around my apartment and started to drive to bars with the intention of cutting myself off at two drinks but often rationalizing a third or fourth beer because it was a "light" one.

The classmate whose marriage was crumbling shot me a look of concern from across the room. "You're still drinking?" he asked. Several heads turned toward me. The instructor stepped off to my left, crossing his arms, forcing me to look at the man confronting me.

I shrugged. "Yeah, but I stopped driving."

"But what happens when you find yourself in a situation when you've had a few drinks and you already drove there?"

I looked up to the instructor for help. He didn't flinch.

"I just won't do it," I said.

I could hear my voice rising as I scanned the room of disappointed faces. Only one of those faces was around my age. Like in AA, most of them were men. I stared down at the table for a moment, worried why none of these people looked like me.

I never told my mother about my DUI. I didn't think she'd understand. Keeping this from her was especially painful since she called me every other day, wanting to know what I was up to. And what I was up to was not worth reporting. While I'd parlayed my internship at *LA Magazine* into paid freelance work as a researcher, not long after, I was let go under a new editor in chief. My days were a slog of alcohol classes, packing to-go orders, and finding the nearest bar with the cheapest drink special.

"Wassup?" I answered one afternoon as I picked at a hole in my bedroom carpet.

"Are you busy?"

Usually, her tone was eager. She wanted to feel connected to my LA life but only in a new, fun, *Sex and the City* trailer kind of way. But today, the conversation spotlight was not on me.

"Maybe you want to sit down for this," she said.

I was already sitting. I sat up straighter. "What's going on?"

She told me she had missed her mammogram appointment one of the times she was in the hospital over the past year. She hadn't rescheduled it until now. And they had found a lump. And it was cancerous. Despite all my mother's illnesses, it never crossed my mind she'd get something else, something as serious sounding as cancer.

"What does this mean?" I asked.

"I'll be fine," she said.

"What stage is it?"

She said she wasn't sure. I knew that stage one was treatable and that stage four was terminal. I also knew that the doctor had surely given her a number, and for whatever reason, she wasn't telling me what this number was.

"I'm having a mastectomy," she said.

"Does that mean it spread?"

"I don't think so. I just don't want to take the chance it'll spread."

As I often did with my mother, I had so many more questions: *Will the surgery get everything? Will there be chemo? Will there be radiation? You'll be OK, right?* But I felt I had to choose my questions carefully if I wanted to get any information at all.

"Of course, I'll be OK," she told me.

"Should I come home, you know, for the surgery?"

"No, it'll be fine. It's already scheduled for next week."

That her surgery was so soon implied she had kept this news from me for a while. Or that her doctors were acting fast because removing the cancer was urgent. Which was not a good sign. But the speed of it all gave me an excuse not to get a ticket home and sit front row as my mother grew more frail and feeble. Because if I was there to see it, I might just guilt myself into staying in Hawai'i for good.

"You sure, you're sure?" I said one more time like a good daughter would.

"Yes, yes, I'm sure."

I could hear it in her voice that she wasn't sure. I didn't press further.

While the universe seemed to be telling me to give up and go home, I didn't want to be the kind of local who couldn't hack it on the continent. My friends who'd moved away for college told me about how they'd join Hawai'i clubs, making friends with other locals they'd normally have little in common with and throwing lū'au, which they had never done when they actually lived in the islands. I had always thought that was silly—if you were going to stick to what was familiar and not branch out, what was the point of moving away at all? There were other locals I'd known from the Hawai'i nightlife scene who'd moved away, who wanted to trade a lazy beach day for power walking among the skyscrapers but who came back after a few years—the winters in New York City were too brutal, the work in San Francisco too unpredictable, rents everywhere more expensive than living at home. Many, though, just missed their 'ohana, the welcoming culture, the easy access to the ocean. I believed I was different. With my nearly all-black wardrobe and anxious energy, I was built for the opportunities and challenges of a city. I would persevere and subvert the norm.

But in all fairness, I actually missed Hawai'i, or I missed the ease of my life there, which was ironic considering that ease was why I'd left. I yearned to just mindlessly grab a teri beef sandwich on my way to work like I used to or stop at the bank to deposit my tips without ever planning the best time to do these things just to fill the minutes. I now had this festering in my na'au that arose out of nowhere. I felt it nagging me to look over there, past my shoulder, and attend to something, but I had no idea what it was.

Often if I wasn't drinking, or even if I was, I tried to quell that nag with food. When I was growing up, my comfort food was a kamaboko sandwich—two pieces of white bread lathered with mayo and stacked with what can best be described as the fish version of Spam, a Japanese hot-pink-and-white roll otherwise sliced for a saimin garnish. Or comfort was a cheeseburger Happy Meal, which, much like the kamaboko, I ate a lot of during the summer of my parents' separation, when my mother was often holed up in her room. Thirteen years later in LA, I would again reach for the warm, cheese-coated greasiness of a McDonald's Quarter Pounder, or an In-N-Out Double Double, or a Tommy's chili cheeseburger after a long night of drinking. (It wasn't as easy to score fish cake from the city's Japanese markets after midnight.) In those moments, I wouldn't think about the thousand calories of carbs I was consuming on top of the thousand calories of booze already sitting in my body. I was feeling the juicy meat crumbles against the roof of my mouth, the tang of mustard on my tongue, all washed down with a handful of salty fries and the creamy goodness of a chocolate shake. Until the next morning when I would regret it all, pinching my stomach fat, sure that I'd added an extra half an inch just in the previous twelve hours. And then sometimes, with my stomach both upset and growling, I would get in my car and hit the drive-through once again, in hopes of subduing my hangover.

Before arriving in LA, I had what you could call the opposite of fat-kid syndrome. I had been a skinny kid who continued to see myself as thin even when I gained ten pounds every year in college. I'd try on clothes, taking a size six into the dressing room, then going back out for an eight and eventually a ten, and mostly shrugged it off. In Hawai'i, size mattered much less than it did in most of the West. I was surrounded by friends and coworkers and locals of all different shapes and body sizes—flat chests, big curves, thick thighs, scrawny legs, and everything in between. There was no type. There wasn't a lot of talk of dieting or feeling guilty about eating deep-fried chicken katsu and a mound of rice for lunch.

But in LA, people talked about what they did and didn't eat quite often. They let you know they felt bad about eating a bagel because it was "all carbs" or ordered a salad for lunch to offset the dessert they had the night before. The messaging was clear: put as few calories into your body as possible, or revel in shame.

I started to scrutinize my body more—my wide hips, my rubbing thighs, my clavicle that did not protrude above my neckline like so many other LA women's. Mong and I often commiserated over our weight, talking about how we wished we could drop ten pounds, maybe fifteen, and then two hours later, we'd be manically eating day-old pizza. It reminded me of that classic eating-disorder study I'd learned about in college: after American television came to Tahiti in the '90s, the pinnacle of popularity for shows like *Beverly Hills 90210* and *Melrose Place*, eating disorders rose drastically among teen girls; 15 percent reported inducing vomiting to control their weight, compared to 3 percent three years prior. Not only were those shows filmed in Los Angeles, but they also took place in Los Angeles.

But the meal that I craved most, the one that reminded me most of home, was plate lunch. A basic plate lunch consists of two scoops of white rice, a scoop of mayo-heavy macaroni salad (locals love a "salad" with mayo), and a salty meat product (char siu pork, kalua pig, shoyu chicken). Plate lunches can be traced back to the sugar plantations in the late 1800s, when workers of various ethnicities would bring their

Local

dinner leftovers, with extra rice added for filler, in bento boxes for lunch. By the 1930s, lunch wagons popped up near plantations serving similar versions but on paper plates. Now, you can find a plate lunch drive-in or hole-in-the-wall on just about every other commercial block in the islands—it's quick, affordable, and fills you up good.

My dad, a laborer who practically lived in his truck, was big into the convenience of plate lunch; I never saw my mother order one. But it was mostly with my friends that I hunched over a Styrofoam container, shoveling greasy meat and mac salad into my mouth: The kalbi plate from Gina's we devoured before going to a punk show, or the Portuguese sausage, eggs, and rice we ate from Zippy's once it was over. The chicken katsu and teri chicken we split at L&L Drive-Inn, chatting about the cute boy a table over and joking about which one of us would have to settle for his less attractive friend. Over plate lunch was where we complained about our parents yelling at us for being "stupid" when we did or wore something they didn't like and where we plotted our evenings, summers, adulthood—our wide, vast future.

In the early aughts, there were several plate-lunch places in LA County, but most were on the southern outskirts. Mong told me she'd heard there was a King's Hawaiian Bakery in Torrance, about thirty-five miles away, and the very next Saturday morning, we were on our way. The entire drive there, we planned what we would order and how we would eat breakfast (Portuguese sausage!) and then take home a plate of katsu curry or huli huli chicken for dinner. While King's resembled an outdated restaurant in Honolulu Airport more than a local mom-and-pop drive-in, the people working there appeared to be legit locals. It's hard to describe how you know another local outside of Hawai'i when you see one—sure, there's a mixed ethnic vibe, the unassuming way they carry themselves, a glint of aloha in the eye—but you just know.

"Are you from Hawai'i? We're from Hawai'i," Mong asked our waitress as soon as she arrived at our table.

"Yeah," she said, smiling. "Makiki. Wen' McKinley High School. You? Where you from?"

"Kaimukī," Mong said, "and Kalihi." She pointed at me.

"Ho, Kalihi, huh? No mess aroun'!"

"Nope!" I said, equally proud and relieved she didn't ask what a haole girl was doing in Kalihi.

After we gave her our order ("You girls stay hungry!"), Mong and I sat there quiet but giddy with the anticipation of children eager to open presents on Christmas morning. Unlike with my high school friends, we didn't make plans or commiserate about boys; we did these things all day long. When our plates finally arrived, I didn't waste any time. I immediately went for a slice of Portuguese sausage, puncturing the grilled meat into the yolk of my eggs. For my next bite, I put a forkful of mac salad on another sausage slice. I closed my eyes and moaned. Across from me, Mong was gathering the perfect bite of hamburger, gravy, yolk, and rice from her loco moco. Between us was a side of Portuguese sweet-bread French toast drowning in syrup and a plate of Spam musubi—a hunk of Spam over a ball of rice, wrapped in seaweed. The only words we said to each other the entire meal were, "God, this is so good."

Twenty minutes later, we were burping our way back to North Hollywood. We complained about our stomachs feeling heavy, how we would skip breakfast tomorrow to make up for today's calories. But in that King's restaurant booth, I wasn't thinking about who I had to be or what I was supposed to look like. I was soothed, dreaming about the katsu I'd have for dinner.

Foreign Bodies

In a big city full of transplants, you're often reduced to where you're from and what dream you're pursuing: *Hi, I'm Jessica, a writer but not a screenwriter, from Hawai'i.* My only gig after the magazine, though, was writing unpaid CD reviews for a free paper found on random street corners. Where I was from was more interesting.

I was often greeted with, "Do you hula? Do you surf?"

"Nope, nope, and I never went to the beach much, either," I'd add for shock value.

But to be fair, when I started bartending and moved to the front of the restaurant, I had just as many questions and stereotypes to run by my coworkers, many of whom were from the Midwest: "Your family sat around an actual dinner table every night, together?"

"Did you have any friends who weren't white?" I once asked a coworker after looking at their prom photos. One former high school footballer told me that in his small town, families stood outside of their houses to watch the team run drills through their neighborhood. Their childhoods seemed even more American pie to me than anything my television allowed me to imagine.

And while continental America, particularly white America, was somewhat exotic to me, I had a love-hate relationship with being exoticized myself. On the one hand, I fit none of the island cliches ("Talking to you, you'd think people in Hawai'i never ate fruit or enjoyed being outside," one coworker told me), but on the other, it was clear that it was cool to be from Hawai'i; it was unexpected ("You get to go home to Hawai'i, how lucky!" others would say).

With my front-of-the-house coworkers, I instead chose to seize upon our similarities: our shared state of limbo, our waiting for a creative future that we were mostly optimistic was going to pan out—at least when we weren't bombarded with thoughts of not being good enough. In the meantime, we would pass the hours with booze and bodies. I had pushed aside any discomfort around my drinking that the DUI classes had stirred up. Now, my calendar was full most nights after work, and after four vodka sodas, someone would inevitably ask, "What are you doing tomorrow?" guaranteeing my next-day afternoons wouldn't be lonely, either. Twenty-three was an age when folks would actually follow through on their drunk plans because it was better than moping around on the couch twelve hours later with a hangover. Did I want to go to a Dodgers game? *Yes*. Did I want to check out some graffiti show in Japantown? *Yes*. Did I want to meet up at Pride and then dance the night away at Micky's? *Yes* and *yes*.

In LA, I could sort of blend between worlds—with my dark features, many thought I was Latina, and yet I was also pale enough for white people to bash immigrants in front of me. It was jarring to hear some of my front-of-the-house coworkers talk of sealing the border when we worked closely with people who had crossed it for a number of reasons. I questioned how they could understand ethnic diversity or immigrant struggles, having grown up around so little of either, and in return, they questioned my patriotism, having grown up so isolated in Hawai'i. Sometimes I would feel dumb for my lack of knowledge of American history or even geography.

But I also realized being from Hawai'i gave me a special advantage: I valued my openness. It would take me much longer to figure out that being too open came at a price.

"Hang loose" was the unofficial motto growing up in Hawai'i. It was a slogan seen on T-shirts in bubble letters above a hand with the thumb and pinkie out, making shaka. It meant not getting too upset about things, too invested, too political. It wasn't worth it. Hanging loose was a self-fulfilling cycle—easier to do the more you didn't question, argue, or analyze.

In this way, my LA friends were correct, to a point: with Hawai'i being so far removed and culturally different from the rest of America, we didn't worry too much about what was going on in the contiguous United States, much less the world. And what we did know was often passed to us through an influential grown-up who had a pre-formed opinion or through pop culture. In middle school, I was aware that the AIDS crisis was devastating gay communities because it was talked about on MTV's *The Real World*, but I didn't realize how it was ignored by governments for years before it reached my consciousness. I knew we had entered the Gulf War during my eighth-grade year, but I couldn't tell you what it was about other than fighting an evil dictator, as one teacher put it. From television and movies, I'd heard a lot about the crack epidemic, as if it was only an inner-city "Black thing," but I had no idea that white people were the majority of crack-cocaine users, that they didn't just do "glamorous" drugs like powdered cocaine. Meanwhile, there wasn't a local family that didn't know at least five people touched by our own "ice," or crystal meth, crisis, who had gone through stints of jail time, homelessness, and scattered employment.

You didn't hear much about ice or poverty in the local news, though, unless it was connected to crime. On the TV screens in both my mother's and father's homes, clear-skinned hapa newscasters mostly gave updates about construction and traffic in their sweet, auntie-like cadence, the weatherman chiming in occasionally with a surf report.

The national news that followed often felt too serious and somber to pay attention to. War, hunger, and murder were for adults.

But while I was in college, there was a Kanaka activist who made the news and stood out for refusing to just hang loose. Haunani-Kay Trask, a UH professor and founding director of the university's Center for Hawaiian Studies, demanded that people open their eyes and start paying attention to problems in the islands. She was bold and fearless; dressed in a kīkepa, or Hawaiian sarong; and always had an earful for camera crews and the local government. She called out the militarization of the islands, the tourism industry, the privilege of haole people; she demanded sovereignty. "Our culture can't just be ornamental and recreational. That's what Waikīkī is," she once said. "Our culture has to be the core of our resistance. The core of our anger. The core of our mana. That's what culture is for."

What most people said about her, both in my own home and around campus, was that she was too loud, too much. "She's just making trouble" was a common refrain. I asked my father once what he thought of sovereignty, and he said it was too late for that. "How we gonna go back?" he said, which was a typical response from locals. Activists weren't demanding the demolition of Burger Kings and movie theaters, though—they wanted the government to officially recognize that their land had been taken, restore what was owed, and then step out of the way and let the Kānaka govern themselves, like other indigenous people around the world have asked of their colonizers.

Trask fought in the traditions of other wāhine activists like Loretta Ritte, who, with her husband, Walter, brought attention to the military's occupation of Kahoʻolawe, and Moanikeʻala Akaka, who fought for Hawaiians who'd been kicked out of farmlands to make way for high-end subdivisions and from ceded trust lands to make way for airport runways. In more recent years, Akaka and the Rittes also actively fought against the construction of the Thirty Meter Telescope to be built on Maunakea, the first-born child of Papa and Wākea and the final resting place of many Kanaka ancestors. After decades of legal battles that ended with a go-ahead from the Supreme Court of the State of Hawaiʻi, construction of the massive telescope was to begin in 2019, but more than a thousand people camped on the sacred mountain, shielding it with their bodies. When the police came to take them away, it was the kūpuna, or elders, like the Rittes, who held the front line. The images from the protest are incredibly powerful and heartbreaking—police officers, many of whom were Kanaka Maoli and part of this community, look pained as they removed their elders, carrying them off in wheelchairs and putting them into police vehicles. The kūpuna's actions were peaceful, moving, clear. But hanging loose did not serve them. They had to make waves.

Aloha is a very real, very powerful thing—a force of love and gratitude you can feel in the breeze, in the ocean, and as you bite into laulau made by a friend. In fact, aloha ʻāina, or love of the land, is at the heart of sovereignty. Aloha ʻāina is what guided Pele, Hiʻiaka, and the many other akua and mortal Kānaka who did not just play nice and allow things to happen, who instead stood up for the land. Aloha should be reserved for what gives you sustenance, what grounds you, what provides you with connection and healing. Unlike what the tourist industry would have you believe, aloha should not be watered down to a pleasantry granted to anyone who stumbles upon cheery Natives. It should not be equated to a blanket niceness. Niceness isn't an effective solution for when situations get complicated or when the sacred gets disrespected.

I've often wondered what would happen if we, as locals, engaged in tensions more, if we allowed ourselves to be uncomfortable. What if we spoke up to ask hard questions, acknowledge that things are not always sunny and equal and chill? What if we dug into what makes us agitated about the Hawaiian activists' message—a reminder of what we have lost, a call to care for the ʻāina—instead of dismissing it? It feels more dangerous to believe the simplistic slogans, to become the one-dimensional hula dancers welcoming everyone with open arms. History has shown that it wouldn't hurt us to be more skeptical of strangers and ideas that might mean us harm.

In May 2001, I got a phone call from an acquaintance in Hawai'i. Daniel was a friend of a friend of mine, and he had just gotten into law school in LA. I didn't know much about him other than the CliffsNotes: he was polite, smart, decent looking, a little rascal. I also knew, because we all came from an island, that he'd recently been caught cheating on his longtime girlfriend—and that was a big reason why he'd chosen a school away from Hawai'i. He called to ask if he could crash for a few days while he looked for a place. Sure, I said, we had a couch.

The evening that Daniel showed up at our place, I gave him the quick-and-easy tour: here is a blanket for the secondhand IKEA sofa I got for free, the one extra towel you can use, and the packets of instant saimin noodles. "Help yourself to whatever you can find to eat," I said as I left him in the kitchen. On the counter lay our Relska jug and a jar of swirled peanut butter and jelly.

He opened and closed the cabinet doors. "What kind of stuff do you girls have to cook with?" he asked.

"You mean like pots and pans?"

"Yeah." He laughed. "I like to cook."

The next afternoon, Daniel came home with more bags of groceries than Mong and I usually bought for a month. He asked what time Mong would be home. Like me, Daniel had worked in restaurants throughout college. Unlike me, he had learned a few things about preparing food. That night, he made us poached salmon in a balsamic reduction. But first, he served a mushroom risotto and grilled asparagus. For dinner, Mong and I usually heated up meat loaf that Jorge would sneak me from the restaurant or grazed on day-old muffins that Mong brought back from one of her three jobs, this one at a nonprofit café to benefit homeless youth living with HIV.

By the time Daniel brought out the chocolate lava cake, we had uttered "oh my god" so many times, it was like a symphony.

"Just repay me in beer," he told us. And with that, we took him to our local dive, the one where I'd met Robbie and that often felt heavy with the unloaded burdens of work (or not finding work), but the place seemed uproarious when Daniel loudly bought the bar a round of Jäger shots.

The next week, we went for drinks again, reminiscing about old pals and haunts we shared back on O'ahu. Nights we stayed in, the three of us watched bad movies and ate popcorn with kaki mochi, the rice crackers we'd sprinkle into our movie tubs in Hawai'i. One day, I even caught Daniel rehanging a picture frame I'd sloppily dangled on a stripped screw.

As Daniel perused online ads for his own place during the week—and then the next week, and the next as he continued to stay with us—we started discussing getting a three-bedroom together. "Look at this one," he said one afternoon, scooting up next to me on the couch where I was lying and watching my mother's beloved *General Hospital*. "It's right off Hollywood Boulevard."

On the way there, we must have passed four Scientology centers. When we pulled up to the building, the elementary school across the street had just let out, and hundreds of screaming kids jammed the sidewalk. The elevator up to the apartment smelled like rotten socks. No matter. It was out of the goddamn Valley. We were close to the action on Cahuenga Boulevard. It was another fresh start.

We let Daniel take us to Hollywood.

It did not take long for us to realize that our twenty-five-unit building was full of twentysomethings who had also moved in for the cheap rent and central location. In the apartment below us were the artists from Philly, who edited short films for cash and were always down to chill. By the elevator were William and Tammy from New Orleans, who did Lord knows what for work but who were always happy to rage. Every month, there was a new set of folks moving in, chasing dreams and highs—the rock cowboys from Texas, the scruffy sculptors from Minneapolis, the nine-to-five threesome from New England that seemed more refined than the rest of us. Mong and I, and Daniel when he was around, were the aloha committee, sure to meet them all, offering leftover foods from our various workplaces. We relished being the "Hawaiian crew," telling neighbors to leave their shoes at the door, being asked how to properly enunciate *karaoke* (*ka-da-o-kay*), or slipping into casual Hawaiian lingo ("I'll come by when I'm pau with work").

When people would call us "the Hawaiians," we'd smile and nod most of the time ("Dat's us!"), but sometimes I'd school them on the nuances of the term. "It's not like being Californian," I'd say. "People who live in Hawai'i are not Hawaiian; they're locals. You don't call people Hawaiian unless they are Native Hawaiian, a.k.a. people with Native Hawaiian ancestry." Then I'd let them know I was both: a local and "a little Native Hawaiian." It still felt necessary to quantify my Hawaiianness.

Blood quantum, or the amount of "Native blood" a person has, is a touchy subject among indigenous groups. In Kanaka tradition, you are Kanaka no matter "how much" Kanaka you are. It's a culture that depends on kinship and genealogy, on an inclusive community of tradition, on being rooted to the 'āina. *Blood quantum*, meanwhile, is a legal term created by governments to be exclusive, to restrict who is able to stake a claim on the land these governments promised to indigenous groups after they stole it from them.

In Hawai'i, any talk of being a quarter or one-sixteenth Native Hawaiian (as opposed to being simply "Native Hawaiian") stems from these restrictions. In 1920, when Hawai'i was still a territory, the Kanaka birth rate was below the national level and Native Hawaiians had a higher death rate than any other minority group in the United States, prompting Congress to hold hearings to discuss a "Hawaiian rehabilitation" program. While these hearings were supposed to lay out whether and which Hawaiians were eligible for homestead lands—leased plots of land meant to encourage reproduction and repopulation—they quickly devolved into racial hypothesizing. For instance, A. G. M. Robertson, a former judge and not a scientist, testified how Hawaiian blood was "absorbed" into white blood, and therefore someone who's one-fourth Hawaiian can assimilate into whiteness and shouldn't qualify for homestead land. It was the 100-percenters that were the poor, inherently disadvantaged "aboriginals" that needed rehabilitating, or so the reasoning went. In the end, Congress agreed there needed to be quantification—the Hawaiian Homes Commission Act set aside two hundred thousand acres of land for Kānaka who had at least "50 percent Hawaiian blood." A century and many generations later, the half-blood rule remains.

Not that this land has been handed over gracefully, or completely, even to those who qualify. Since 1921, only ten thousand Native Hawaiians have been allotted homestead land; more than twenty-eight thousand remain on a waitlist.

When growing up, I heard people quantify their Hawaiianness but never do the same for any other part of their ethnic makeup past the hapa, or halfway, mark; no one ever said, "I'm one-thirty-second Chinese." The Hawaiian blood-quantum law, whether we realized it or not, has had long-reaching effects on how locals see Kānaka and how Kānaka see ourselves.

When people in Hawai'i asked what I was, I often offered up my fraction of Kanaka, as if to say, *I belong here but only this much.* On the continent, though, I wasn't sure how much Hawaiian I was entitled to be. Daniel was more Kanaka than me, or at least he seemed more local, with his dark skin and sun-kissed surfer hair. I felt more "Mainland" with my fair complexion and Urban Outfitters sale-rack thermal—and yet we were also from the same kinship, the same culture, one that was found nowhere else but in the islands.

"If you don't surf or like the sun, what kind of Hawaiian are you?" a neighbor once asked.

"Not a good one, I guess," I answered, laughing. But I was only half-joking—I often felt like an "illegitimate" Hawaiian. It wouldn't be until much later that I'd learn about these blood-quantum histories. You could say colonization had worked as intended: erase the Kanaka out of their person and their land—if not through literal death, then by immersion into whiteness.

After my DUI was settled, my dad stopped calling so much. Our conversations were usually short, and sometimes Shellee would get on the phone, and we'd laugh about all the dieting customers I waited on who'd order salads without croutons or dressing. But mostly they wanted to make sure I was all right. I assumed financially all right, so I told them I was making better tips now that I was bartending and serving, and that business was so good, the restaurant even opened up a new wine room. "Good, girlie," my dad said, and with that, I was free to end the phone call.

My mom was more persistent with her outreach. She had undergone her mastectomy, but the cancer had spread to her lymph nodes, and she was undergoing chemotherapy. Radiation would come next. I came to dread the phone ringing, asking her how she was feeling. She would say she was OK, but her voice revealed she was exhausted.

I started to purposely leave my cell phone on vibrate so that I wouldn't have to hear the tiredness in her tone. Sometimes I'd call her back minutes before arriving at work. "I gotta park the car. Talk later?" But more often, I let her messages pile up until I became annoyed by the number of missed calls. "Why did you have to leave the same message three times? Don't you know that if I didn't hear one message, then I didn't hear any of the other ones?" I lectured her one afternoon.

"I don't know how these cell-phone things work," she said in her girlish voice.

"Mom, you're not that old. You have a television. You know what a cell phone is," I replied. "We don't need to talk every day, do we?"

"No." She sighed. "I just miss you."

On evenings when I wasn't at the restaurant, I wandered down the hall and knocked on William's door and he'd let me in, a wad of dip behind his smile and half a pack of beer in his fridge. Eventually, one of the Philly guys would show up with a bottle of Jim, and shots slid down our throats as we made plans to head to Cahuenga.

Our favorite stop was the Beauty Bar, a faux-1950s beauty salon trimmed in gold and accented in powder blues. There, we stepped up our game to fit the part. Two cosmos for Mong and me, an apple martini for Tammy—make it one more for Daniel—a round of Heinekens for the other dudes, and—why not?—a round of whiskey shots as well. Drinks in hand, we started off as a big cluster, but by the second and third drink, we sectioned off into smaller and smaller ones, until we were just yelling in another person's ear, maybe a stranger's. Often, I was with Mong, the two of us either dancing or complaining about how the brooding guy in the corner wasn't noticing us.

Even though Daniel was trying to work things out with his ex, he was usually paired up with a woman. Sometimes it was our neighbor Tammy, her head tilted up at him as he traced his fingers down the back of her top. I was in awe of how quickly Daniel could get girls to make out with him. How in one instant he was chatting up a woman, then drawing her close, getting handsy all over the dance floor, and then excusing himself for another drink. When I joked with him about it ("fast work, dude"), he'd give me a bonus detail like "and her tits are firm, too," and I'd shake my head or roll my eyes. With sober Daniel, you could see in the pause before he spoke that he wanted to be the careful, quintessential Mr. Aloha. But with drunk Daniel, the pressure to be pleasant went completely out the window.

My first one-night stand was with a guy from out of town. I met him at an '80s night. I was too drunk to drive home, so I asked a friend to drop this stranger and me off at my apartment. We ran up to my room, I unbuttoned my pants, and he went down on me until I came. When I pulled his pants down, he couldn't stay hard. I called him a cab.

My next was a friend of Tammy's, a model. He was in the city for a *Playgirl* shoot. We all went out dancing, the two of us coyly flirting at the edge of the dance floor. When the group of us got back to the apartment building, everyone else went to bed, and the model came with me to mine. He gently kissed my shoulders, my neck. His face was soft. Inside of me, he moved slowly. Even when he came, his eyes, his cheeks didn't tense up; he was relaxed. As soon as he pulled himself out, he put his jeans back on. "I should get back to Tammy's before she notices," he said. I nodded.

"Totally," I said, even though part of me hoped he would stay. Still, it was a great story to tell my friends. "He was definitely qualified to be in *Playgirl*," I bragged.

Daniel and I often joked about our previous night's exploits, a sort of sibling rivalry in the art of luring the opposite sex. One morning, Daniel barged into my room without knocking to see if I wanted to grab breakfast. I was lying in bed, half-awake. A bushel of hand-washed panties was wrapped around the doorknob. "Look at you!" he said, about to grab the doorknob from the inside. "Get some last night?" Obviously, I didn't get "it" eight times, as indicated by the eight pairs of underwear he was referring to. I hadn't had any in over a month. Still, I blushed and played along.

"Why? Jealous?" I asked.

While Daniel and I teased and taunted each other like locker-room buddies, he knew my game was novice and that most of my sights were set on a guy from work who'd come around every once in a while to party with us but then bailed before anyone noticed. "It makes no sense," I whined to Daniel one afternoon over a game of pool at a neighborhood bar. "We're so much alike," I said about my crush.

Daniel walked around the pool table without looking up at me. He aimed to sink the seven in the corner pocket. He missed. "Damn," he muttered.

"Well, what do you think?" I asked, walking around the table to stand directly across from him. "Why doesn't he make a move?" My pool cue thumped against the floor. I was hoping he'd make me feel better and say, "He'll come around," or at least, "His loss."

"Well, some guys just have different standards," Daniel said.

I started to crack a smile, waiting for Daniel to crack one, too, and lay another joking jab. Instead, he turned to face the sports scores on the television screen. I leaned into the table to take my shot. I, too, missed. For the first time, I realized I cared whether Daniel found me attractive or not.

One night, Daniel and I were on our way home with some friends when one of them told me to pull over. She had to puke.

I turned down a residential street and parked the car. My friends scurried out of the back seat and into the night. I rolled out of the car, too, onto some stranger's lawn, the ground spinning beneath me as I closed my eyes. The next thing I knew, Daniel was on top of me. His bleached, shoulder-length hair tickled my nose. His long, lean body fell against mine. "Daniel, what are you doing?" I asked, my eyes still closed. He pried my legs open with his knees. Before I knew it, his tongue was in my mouth.

"What about Julie?" I muttered with his face smashed against mine. I was thinking about his girlfriend, miles away in her own apartment, probably sleeping at this hour.

"Are you guys ready to go?" one of my friends called out. I pushed Daniel off me, and we hurried toward them. Once in the streetlight, she shot me an "oh boy, what have you gotten yourself into again" smirk. I smirked back, preferring to be seen as naughty rather than uncomfortable and confused.

When we got home, I went straight to my bedroom and sat on the edge of my bed. I wasn't ready to go to sleep, but I didn't want to go back down and run into Daniel. Soon enough, he was in my doorway. He wanted to pick up where he left off on the lawn. He wanted, I could tell, to drop the subject of his girlfriend. I looked into his black eyes as he walked closer, hoping he'd flash me his dimples and reassure me that we were just having fun. If he could somehow explain to me why two roommates who weren't really attracted to each other were about to muddle several relationships, then I wouldn't have to explain it to myself. But he said nothing, and I gave in to my desire to simply feel desired. I let him come over to me on the bed.

I laid my head back on the pillow. My arms surrendered. He unsnapped my blouse with one stroke of his hand. He pinned my wrists behind my head. I turned away. But I didn't stop him. Not yet. First, I let him pull on my shoulder-length curls, brushing my hair aside to suck on my neck. I allowed him to scoop his hands under my back and twist the hook of my bra while I wondered if he'd been harboring lust for me or if he just assumed I would sleep with him because we were drunk enough to break a few rules.

Suddenly, the thought of getting naked with the man I belched with over breakfasts, a man I saw as my older brother and protector, made me want to leap out of bed.

"Daniel, get off," I said, rolling out from under him. "This is weird." He flipped over to look at me, his dark pupils dulled. He didn't even seem to know where he was. He grabbed his pants and shook his head, turning toward the door like he had just come in to get something he'd forgotten.

After he left, I circled my room. I went over to my dresser and took my pajamas out of the drawer. I threw them on the floor. I snapped my shirt back on and peeked out my bedroom door. Daniel's door, only ten feet away, was shut.

I ran downstairs on tiptoes so that he wouldn't hear, out the front door and into the elevator. Someone in the building had to be up, I thought. I got off on the floor below ours, relieved to see the Philly guys' lights on. Two minutes later, I was on the other side of the door with a beer in my hand.

When I thought of my Kanaka ancestors being sexually uninhibited before the missionaries and the colonizers, I didn't truly understand what that inhibition meant. I had been influenced by the extremes of Christian moral codes and the explicit highlights of television hookups. How wild it must have been to instead have been raised in a community that could tap into both their carnal and intimate desires, letting them rise to the surface for exploration, free of moral constraint. A romantic encounter where you learned to trust your partner on such a journey and still center your own pleasure was beyond my imagination. It must have gone hand in hand with being rooted in the present, something I had little practice in.

To me, sexual liberation only existed in terms of breaking free from the Western, Christian expectations of being a chaste, compliant woman. I wanted to be a woman who wasn't told how to behave, who took control, who was seen as cool for being sexual. But even my definition of liberation was twisted—it wasn't the freedom to figure out what I desired but the power to use my body to feel like I had conquered someone. Liberation was winning.

When I was on top and my partner was seconds away from release, I'd stare at their eyelids, willing them to open. I wanted them to look at me and know that I was the one giving this to them. But that rarely happened. On the bottom, in a more vulnerable position, I didn't want eye contact. I wanted to feel them enter me. I wanted to feel anything, even if it was pain, so long as it wasn't emptiness.

But the best part about sex, for me, was always the minutes, hours before the sex itself. My flirtations returned, my desires seen and ensnaring another's. The knowledge that I had snagged this man's attention and made him mine, even just for an evening.

My next intended one-night stand, in some ways, ended up a failure. He returned again and again.

Ben, a stuntman from Iowa, was a new guy from work. We flirted like high schoolers. One night I noticed he had a milk stain on his apron from frothing a cappuccino. "Did you get excited?" I asked, lowering my eyes to the splat near his crotch.

"Only for you," he said, smiling.

At the Christmas party, I decided I was going to have Ben. I sat down across from him at one of the tables and pointed to a roll of candy, a gag gift he'd opened from his Secret Santa. "I want one," I told him.

He flipped an orange candy into his mouth. "Come and get it." I leaned across the table, cluttered with empty martini glasses. I put my lips to his and stole the candy in one lickety-swoop.

His eyes widened. "Here," he said, popping a second candy into his mouth, "have another one."

Ben came back to my apartment that night. We were in the living room for five minutes before I led him to my bedroom. He stopped in the doorway. I kept walking toward the bed. I stripped down to my underwear and crawled underneath the sheets, my cinematic way of letting him know he could have me. He didn't budge. He raked his fingers through his blond hair, unsure if a girl who had just consumed seven fruity martinis and stumbled up the stairs was what he wanted at that moment. He got into bed, and we fooled around until I fell asleep.

We started to grab drinks after work, and a few nights a week, he'd come home with me. We made out, groped, cuddled some, but I didn't understand why he hesitated to have penetrative sex. If sex wasn't the thing that kept him coming back, then maybe it was the tease of it, I assumed.

The nights Ben and I didn't work together, neither of us called the other. He was a bit immature (he called vaginas "kootzers") and liked to keep conversations breezy (it was unclear if he felt deeply about anything other than Iowa and football). I didn't know if he was dating anyone else, but the way he didn't rush out of bed in the morning, lingering to joke around, putting all his weight on me in a move he called "the crusher," how some days we even got dressed and grabbed huevos rancheros, was enough for me. Clarity on our status would have opened me up to rejection. That he kept showing up, that he made me smile and asked little of me in return, was the best I couldn't ask for.

Unwell

Traditionally, when the Kānaka gave birth, they planted their baby's placenta, along with a new tree, near their home. It was a way to ensure that the tree and child would grow together. New life entwined, anchored.

Since I had already pulled up that anchor and had no plans of returning, my mom decided to uproot her own home to move closer to me.

In the spring of 2002, about a year and a half after I moved to LA, my mom called: she and Ed were moving to California. They'd settled on Temecula, a suburb about ninety miles south and inland of Los Angeles. "But aren't you too sick to move?" I asked. My mom was practically bedridden at that point, her cancer elevated to stage three—a fact I was able to get out of her. They wanted to move, she said, and Ed had chosen Temecula because it was affordable. "But is it a good idea to change all your doctors now?" I asked.

"The new doctors will have all my records," she said. "It'll be fine! We can finally live out our California dreams."

This was possibly the most delusional thing my mom had ever said. More likely, Ed needed my help. My mother surely wished to have me around. But no one said any of these things, making it easier for me not to consider their true reasons for moving. None of us—not Ed, not my mom, not I—had ever broached the idea that she was dying. And we weren't going to start now.

I could chart the demise of my mother's health by a few different paths.

She'd always had that clumsy streak, but her penchant for accidents and ailments escalated soon after marrying Ed. In 1989, age forty-five and freshly remarried, she tumbled down the stairs outside of her classroom and hobbled around in a full leg cast for six weeks, with Ed driving her to school and helping her up the stairs to her classroom. In 1990, at age forty-six, she fell off the edge of the bathtub she'd been standing on to shut a window and wore a neck brace for two months, with Ed putting her comfortably on her pillow every night. In 1991, at age forty-seven, she took a spill down the school stairs again; this time, they decided it made more financial sense for her to buy her own pair of crutches. In 1993, at age forty-nine, she was diagnosed with fibromyalgia. In 1994, at age fifty, sciatica. In 1995, at age fifty-one, lupus. In 1997, at age fifty-three, she tripped over a curb in the parking lot of her favorite department store, injured her ankle, and started wearing a special foot brace whenever she walked farther than room to room; Ed was the one to strap the foot brace on her and guide her to the fridge and back. In 1998, at age fifty-four, she formed a pinched nerve in her spine from the fall or from the foot or from sitting in bed because of the foot. In 1999, at age fifty-five, she slipped in the supermarket, falling on her back. In 2000, at age fifty-six, between the foot, the pinched nerve, and the aggravated back, she was using a walker full-time; that same year, she was diagnosed with breast cancer. In 2001, at age fifty-seven, months before she moved, she had an eight-hour back surgery, but it was unsuccessful, and afterward, she needed a brace to even sit upright. On top of chauffeuring her to numerous doctor's appointments, Ed was the one making food runs and pill pickups, planning his workouts and golf games around my mother's naps and when she got hungry. He was the one helping her in and out of the tub and organizing her medicine cabinet so that when she wobbled in there, she could brush her teeth and wash her face efficiently. My dad wouldn't have stuck around—the few times she did injure herself during their marriage, I don't remember him being there to help; he wasn't good with weakness—but Ed, who was dutiful and retired, was there. He had committed to living out their lives together, and I believe he still hoped that was possible.

But there's another through line I could draw that coincided with my mother's decline. Clumsiness is a result of the mind detached from the body. Shame is the mind preoccupied with trauma. Trauma has an effect on the immune system, particularly inflammation, worsening disease. I think about how swallowing a massive secret like giving up a child, locking it in the pit of her gut for thirty-five years, must've weighed on my mother's body. I picture knots forming in her stomach, toxins accumulating, organs stressed. Every time my mother suffered silently—hiding away her pregnancy, divorcing my dad, who had fathered a child with another woman—I picture another mass of stress, another dose of toxin, accumulating on top of the last.

Then there is a third timeline to follow, another track of my mother's silent suffering: my move out of her house, my less frequent visits, my relocating to another state. All my attempts to push my mother away surely didn't make her feel any better, in her mind or body.

After my mother and Ed arrived in Temecula in April of 2002, I settled on visiting her once a week on my day off. On a typical Wednesday, I woke up late, having gone out the night before. I had a leisurely bowl of cereal and watched *The View*, a show I didn't even care about. I got into my car just before noon.

One Wednesday, about thirty minutes into my drive, I had to pull over in the emergency lane to puke out my car door. The diner just off her exit had a nice bathroom where I could rinse out my mouth and run my fingers through my curls. I didn't want to hear my mom tell me that my hair was out of control.

As soon as I opened the door to her townhome, my mom called out from her room, "Jessica, is that you?" knowing full well it was me because they never had any other visitors.

"Yes," I yelled back, kicking off my sandals and taking a sharp turn not into her bedroom but into the kitchen.

At the sound of my voice, Ed hurried out from the spare room—informally his bedroom since my mom never left the bed in "their room"—grabbed his keys, and walked out with a nod and a terse hello. We were in a relay race to care for my mom, and I had been handed the baton.

In her kitchen, I slapped a Kraft single on a slice of white bread, a snack my mother had taught me to make for myself as a kid. For four minutes, I stared at the toaster oven, watching the cheese bubble until the corners turned brown.

In her room, my mother was on her back, straining her head to look up at me. "That looks good," she said, my plate hovering above eye level.

"It's just toast, Mom." With my one free hand, I reached down to give her a light hug—one arm on her shoulder—so as not to disrupt her back. Brushing aside her bangs, still slightly stiff from yesterday's hairspray, I kissed her forehead and walked around to lie next to her on this new king-size bed.

The air conditioner was set to a moderate freeze, a crack in her bedroom curtains revealing the relentless brightness of the Southern California sun. They had sold their old furniture before the move, and their new stuff looked like they'd pointed to full displays in a chain-store showroom and said, "We'll take that one." It wasn't a modern or classic aesthetic like I would assume my mother would choose but heavy woods and drapery with accents of brown and red. It felt dark, weighted, like a bland medieval castle trapped in a box of drywall. But just like in their Hawai'i home, everything was neat and in place. My mother's bed was made under her. Even though she spent nearly every hour of every day in that bed, never did she get under the covers. Instead, casually strewn across her legs was a throw blanket, as if she could fling it off and leave at any time.

By the time she'd moved away, my mother's life in Hawai'i had been reduced to not much more than what she had in Temecula—a bed, a television, snacks, Ed. But Hawai'i, with its literal rainbows after every light rain shower, had once been an emblem of hope and safety for her: it's where she ran to when she was my age and didn't feel like she belonged; it's where she found her kuleana in front of the classroom and where she learned that people would accept her, even if she never felt entirely comfortable enough to expose all her layers. Once retired and in poor health, though, she was shut out from the familiar ways in which Hawai'i had healed her. And yet in both Makakilo and Temecula, she still got dressed every day, her hair and makeup done, too, as if, maybe, she'd be part of the outside world once again.

In her bedroom, it's not like I was eager to settle in, either. I propped myself up against her headboard, tearing off tiny pieces of bread. I knew once my last bite was eaten, it was time to get into my regular position—back flat, at her level.

Just like when I was in college, *Friends* was always on. Then there was the week's worth of soaps she had taped for me, like I hadn't watched a number of them while lying around my own apartment most afternoons, waiting to go to work. A few hours into our sitcom-and-soaps marathon, my hangover started to recede. That's when remorse started to brew—what did I say to Ben last night? How long did I have to spend in this bed before I could get back into my car? Often, I could override this agitation with other, less loaded worries—what bar I was going to meet my friends at later, when I would make time to do my laundry.

It was clear my mother also needed to break up the time and the refrains playing through her own mind. She asked for a Peppermint Pattie, then, twenty-five minutes later, a Klondike Bar. She needed to go to the bathroom often, and Ed, who was usually back after a few hours away, needed to help me help her.

"Really? Again?" I asked. "But you just went half an hour ago."

"I know, but I gotta go," she said in her tiny voice.

My mom could no longer walk anywhere, even with guidance. Just to get ten feet to the bathroom, I had to pull her soft body to a sitting position using the flaps of the quilted pad on which she lay. She was nearly twice as heavy as she'd been in my childhood, but I did my best not to let the struggle show. Once she was upright, I attached a plastic brace to her front and another to her back, fastening the three belts on each side that held the braces together. As I did this, her girlish eyes widened, and she looked up at me as if to say *thank you, sorry,* or *pretty please.* But I pretended not to see them. I kept my focus on getting the belts tight.

"There, is that good?" I asked, giving it one last unnecessary tug.

"Yes." She was still looking up at me. "Are you growing out your hair?"

I flipped a strand away from my face and kept moving. The next step was getting her into the wheelchair. I lifted the metal arm, sliding her off the bed and into the chair. "Ow, ow, ow," she whimpered, squinting her eyes. I turned my head to the television and watched Joey stick a spoon into a giant vat of jam.

I wheeled my mom to the doorway of the adjoining bathroom and called for Ed. His job was to roll her inside, shut the door, and undress her. My mother wanted to retain her sense of dignity. After twenty-five years, she still wouldn't let me see her naked.

I lay back down. Monica was scolding Joey about eating the jam.

Not even a minute later, my mom yelled she was done.

"Ed, she's done," I yelled, lifting my head from the pillow so that my voice would carry out the bedroom door.

He stomped back in, opened the bathroom door, and shut it behind him. Two minutes and several grunts later, he reappeared with my mom. He pushed her wheelchair the first five feet and then let her roll the other five to the edge of the bed. It was my turn again, this time to go through the whole process of bracing her in reverse.

"What did I miss?" she asked, nodding toward the television. I turned away just as Joey dug into another big hunk of jam.

The funny thing about the trope of the smiley, unshakable local girl is how far it has strayed from the nuanced way my Kanaka ancestors spoke about their emotions, particularly depression and anxiety. *Lu'ulu'u* is to be bowed down with weight, grief, sorrow. *Lauele* is to wander mentally. Depression triggered by an outside circumstance is *loha*, meaning "to fade or wilt." To be filled with so much worry and agitation you can't sleep is to feel *ulukū*. To be overtaken with so much worry that your stomach hurts is *manawahua*.

I didn't have these words for these emotions growing up, though. Like most children of American boomers, I learned that if you're feeling down, buck up and carry on. Do not overshare or be a burden. The connection between physical health and mental well-being was not discussed.

In the island culture around me, though, there were hints that Hawaiians and locals had developed ways to bridge these connections. Lomilomi is a type of therapeutic massage, traditionally learned from your 'ohana, that begins with pule, or prayer, before using the hands, elbows, and forearms to release tension and negative energy throughout the body. If you are ill, seawater is the cure for whatever ails you. Drink some to flush out the toxins from the kidneys and liver and stomach; add a touch of herbs grown in your garden, like ʻōlena, or turmeric, for relieving pain. Surfers will tell you that a dip in the ocean, that first full-body plunge when you enter, is also restorative, alleviating headaches and stresses brought on by daily life. Your body will thank you, too, if you consume a diet grown from the earth—ʻulu, taro, guava, lilikoʻi. These fruits and vegetables, harvested by those who care for the ʻāina, are packed with antioxidants and fiber to keep all systems chugging along.

In LA, there was much talk about wellness, too, but in an à la carte kind of way. Angelenos often pick and choose practices borrowed from indigenous and Eastern cultures—yoga, crystals, tarot, various types of meditation—to get in touch with their bodies and the surrounding world. This mental zen is usually coupled with a physical regimen. The idea is to sculpt and feel at peace with an outward appearance through things like expensive reiki facials paired with a Botox treatment, or hot yoga classes where participants sweat out all their toxins while shedding several pounds of water weight. Here, the focus is less on breathing from your piko and more on the abdominal muscles themselves, squeezing them in for 10-9-8-7 to achieve a six-pack. Not that there's anything wrong with adding a little vanity to a routine of balance. It's the modern way to survive a city that values youth and beauty (Hollywood, baby!) as much as decompressing from those pressures.

In LA, there is also an emphasis on organic and pesticide-free foods, on mineral waters and cleansing potions, as well as a fear of fruits and the sugars, although natural, that come with them. Carbs are the Angeleno's enemy. No banana smoothies (sub green juice) or after-dinner ice cream (only the occasional fro-yo) or any kind of bread (unless that's the only meal you'll consume all day). The goal is to be thin at all costs (people will joke, but they are dead serious)—this is what will bring happiness. It is not to honor and nourish the body each of us is given.

As a woman in LA eager for self-peace and outward validation, I created my own version of anti-wellness wellness. I consumed the Hollywood 48-Hour Miracle Diet, a concoction that was supposed to help you quickly lose four to eight pounds and ironically tasted like Hawaiian Sun juice. *A kickstart will make me feel better about myself,* I believed, and I needed to feel better about something. After those two days, I exclusively ate grilled chicken breasts and salads at the restaurant ("Why you worry about being flaca?" Jorge asked me, shaking his head when my order came in) and tried out whatever exercise classes my coworkers were into (Pilates, yoga, Zumba) because I'd never exercised before and didn't know where to start.

This warped LA version of health also changed my visits with my mother. I started packing gym clothes and a bikini for my afternoons there, hours that were shrinking week by week. I'd show up, say hello, and then spend forty-five minutes swimming and tanning by their community pool, followed by forty-five minutes on the elliptical machine in their gym. Then I bought us fast-food dinners as I always had, only to lie in my mother's bed afterward, my hand on my stomach, sucking the muscles in and out to measure how much it had expanded. I'd count the calories that I consumed all day and subtract from them the workout I did earlier. Then I'd get up to grab an after-dinner candy just to get out of bed again. When I lay back down, I would promise to burn an extra five hundred calories tomorrow, somehow.

One evening, though, I looked over at my mother and noticed the curls falling around her face, spilling onto her pillow. Her eyes, an already-diluted green in color, were watery and glassy as they stared through the television screen, somewhere between the verge of tears and a zen-like plateau. "Tickle my arm," she asked. I inched closer. I told myself I wouldn't disconnect, not this time; I wouldn't turn my mind to calories or treats.

I ran my fingers up and down the loose skin of her arm and put my head on her pillow. Her curls felt soft and springy against my nose. Her mascara was clumpy, her eyeliner flaking from under her lids, applied while lifting her head for a few painful seconds at a time to look into a folding mirror placed on her lap. Near the back of her head, I could see a few wispy hairs sticking out, flattened and tangled from being pressed against her pillow.

That's when I moved into her neck. She smelled of aloe cream, hairspray, and the Oscar de la Renta I used to spray on my teenage wrists. I nuzzled into her shoulder and took a whiff. Then I pulled away. I flipped over and gave her my back. I wanted to breathe in that smell forever, yet it only reminded me that there'd come a time, most likely very soon, when I would struggle to re-create that chemistry from simple memory.

"We all must go alone."

This line from Olomana's 1976 song "Ku'u Home O Kahalu'u" has long haunted me. I listened to the song quite a bit as a teenager, the plucking of one guitar layered over the soft strumming of another. The slow, sorrowful journey through a life past and present. Local boy Jerry Santos was singing about change, "a strange thing that cannot be denied. It can help you find yourself or make you lose your pride. Move with it slowly," he sang, but "please do not hold on to me. We all must go alone."

I discovered the song while flipping through radio stations my senior year in high school, a time when "adulthood" and all its unknowns were just around the corner. It was one of those songs that didn't just *feel* poignant; I knew it was. What I didn't realize then, though, was that it was written during the Hawaiian Renaissance, when Kānaka Maoli were speaking out against the damage wrought by over a hundred years of colonialism. While Kānaka have a bevy of terms to describe sadness, perhaps the greatest-felt and the least-mentioned injury is the generational trauma of being displaced from the 'āina and forbidden from your culture. This is the unresolved grief Hawaiians feel in our bones, the hard-to-pinpoint depression and anxiety that leaves us searching for something we can't quite name. "I remember days when we were younger," the song begins. "We used to catch 'o'opu in the mountain stream. 'Round the Ko'olau hills we'd ride on horseback. So long ago it seems it was a dream."

At the time, I just thought I preferred the "old," sad Hawaiian songs from the '70s to the contemporary Jawaiian jams, with their lower stakes and move-along reggae undertones. Being into music that evoked uglier hidden emotions—the aggro of punk, the mope of goth—I was drawn to songs like "Ku'u Home" because listening to them was like looking straight into the gaping hurt of someone's heart wounds.

There were some obvious clues, however, that my favorite Hawaiian songs were about something weightier than a vague change that the teenage me could tap into. Perhaps the most blatant example is Israel Kamakawiwo'ole's "Hawai'i '78," a call to action written by Mickey Ioane, Clayton Kua, Abe Keala, and Kawika Crowley that Iz originally played with his band, Mākaha Sons of Ni'ihau. In it, he sings about how if our former kings and queens saw what had become of the islands—highways on their sacred grounds, condominiums on the land they unified—"Tears would come from each other's eyes, as they would stop to realize that our people are in great great danger now."

While Iz is best known for his "Over the Rainbow" cover, played in numerous movies and commercials, many of his original songs describe the loss of culture, tradition, and 'āina; he was a Hawaiian sovereignty activist. Santos, meanwhile, said he wrote "Ku'u Home" when he lived in a tiny, fourth-floor walk-up in the Bay Area after scoring a record deal. "I flew the coop, and so the song was about acknowledging who you are and where you come from, what your choices are," he once told *Honolulu* magazine. He called the song "a conversation to my family."

In this context, "We all must go alone" makes sense—a twentysomething making the decision to move away from his beloved Kahaluʻu to chase his dreams, even if his family may not have understood. The choices feel selfish. Loving your home but wanting more feels like a betrayal. The tension of holding both your own ambitions and your parents' expectations is incredibly isolating. But I can only guess it's why artists like Iz and Santos put their feelings into words, sharing them with the world: to pave the journey through pain is to bring it to light.

And yet years later, "We all must go a-loooooone" is the part of "Kuʻu Home" that still stood out to me. The words rang in my head as I thought of my mother, her condition, her inevitable transition out of this life. Then there was my own journey of acceptance that I hesitated to take. The thing was, neither my mother nor I actually wanted to go it alone. But we weren't Santos or Iz. We couldn't expose our vulnerability and admit we needed one another. Instead, we lay close, not quite touching, never acknowledging who we were together or apart, just like we did when I was little.

Occasionally, I'd utilize my journalism skills and try to catch my mom in a "gotcha."

"Would you have been fine staying in Hawaiʻi and not moving to California?" I asked one afternoon as we lay beside each other.

"Yeah, I made my life there," she said. "Hawaiʻi was my home."

I sat up, surprised. "Not Louisiana?"

"No, of course not. I haven't lived there in over thirty years." She paused for a minute before backpedaling on her first statement. "But I was fine moving here, too. This is what Ed and I talked about."

There was the gotcha I was looking for—moving was Ed's idea after all! It was easy for me to blame Ed, the interloper in the already-strained relationship between my mother and me, and make him the bad guy in all that was hard and unsaid. But hearing her admit the move was his idea didn't feel particularly like a win. It made me sad that she was in this new place that wasn't home. That her life had been a set of circumstances she went along with, trying to keep her composure.

If we were all still in Hawai'i, maybe we could have handled this with more peace, I thought. Maybe my mom would have been soothed by the sound of trade winds blowing through the windows. Maybe, despite being embarrassed about her puffy appearance, she would have allowed her old teaching buddies to share a laugh at her bedside. But I also already knew that the sicker she became, the more she had pushed those friends away.

For me, I wondered if a long day in bed with my feeble mother might have been offset by walking through the door of the Kalihi house to find Shellee's smile or my dad's offer for dinner pancakes at Liliha Bakery or the worn-in warmth of my childhood comforter—as opposed to the empty LA apartment I often walked into since Mong and Daniel had become serious in their respective relationships. The hills of Moanalua on the drive back from Makakilo could possibly be more consoling than the constellation of brake lights awaiting me in downtown Los Angeles on my way back from Temecula. My longtime pockets of mana wahine might offer me the support that I craved from the partying, half-coherent neighbors whose doors I knocked on at 1:00 a.m. But there's a better chance I still would have found a way to check out like I always had. I was the one who had run away, after all.

To be fair, Los Angeles is no slouch when it comes to landscape. It is not Manhattan, a city contained on an island that is mostly flat and packed with skyscrapers. LA supports a variety of terrains and climates within its 503 square miles, from the ocean to the desert to the windy canyons. You can't see the mountains or the Pacific from every vantage point like you can in Hawai'i, but old crags and peaks rise up from the City of Angels, too. The ocean, though chillier and less clear, is also there if you want to meditate on its motion. Step outside, and it is the same sun following you around, reminding you that you are alive, if you let it.

When a few of my coworkers first mentioned hiking, I was hesitant, being someone not only disinterested in daylight but also averse to getting dirty. But the plan, as dictated to me, was to get in an hour or so of cardio, then reward ourselves with a boozy brunch. Runyon and Fryman Canyons, and Griffith Park, weren't exactly wild, unexplored treks. The trails were wide and well populated, with dozens of residents with tight bodies and elusive jobs getting in their midday fitness. I didn't stop to pick dandelions or even spend much time taking in the views, but I did like feeling the sun on my face, the strain in my quads as I kicked dirt up the mountain. Following a path required less concentration and coordination than making it through a workout class. Plus, I wasn't completely alone with my mind or trying to silence it. There was conversation to carry me along.

The coworkers I hiked with had become more than just drinking buddies. While they didn't outright acknowledge what a mental mess I was, they did inquire about my mother and ask how I was doing. They looked at me with empathy when I talked about how dependent she was and didn't judge me, even though the subtext of my complaints was that I resented my dying mother's neediness.

Ben continued to come around, too. He also liked to be out of the house, having grown up in a small town where vacations were trips to the state fair and dining out rarely happened. I took him for dim sum in Chinatown and to watch the Latin hip-hop band Ozomatli blow out a small, crowded venue with their horn section. He took me to an "eggs and kegs" party at his favorite sports bar and for a weekend in Santa Barbara, where we dodged pedestrians on a tandem bicycle.

One night, two months into dating, Ben sat down on the edge of his bed and told me why he was hesitant to have sex. He told me he liked me, but he was flying up to Illinois next weekend to take a paternity test. He didn't know whether he was the father of his ex's baby. He thought it was unlikely because they had rebound sex only once after they broke up, before he met me, but his ex wanted to be sure. I didn't feel surprised or betrayed but, rather, relieved. That he had kept this from me for so many weeks, that he had waited until the last minute to tell me, was less important to me than him coming clean. Being scared shitless of the repercussions of sex seemed like a good reason to turn me down.

When he found out he was not the father, our hanging out became more constant. People at work started asking us if we were boyfriend and girlfriend. We giggled, made jokes, didn't directly answer them. We had sex in a movie theater bathroom, on the side of the highway, on top of the bar after work since I had the keys to close the restaurant. I wanted to show him the wait was worth it. I wanted to prove to myself that I was still up for fun and spontaneity.

But while I considered his opening up about the paternity test to be some kind of turning point, we did not necessarily start emotionally inviting each other in. I did not talk about the anxiety that was growing inside of me or my fears about my mother; I couldn't even admit them to myself. Ben and I would chat about our day and gossip about our coworkers, but neither of us discussed our feelings for each other. As a friend once pointed out, Ben had a Zack Morris vibe—the cool blond guy who communicated in one-liners and innuendos. His way of showing me affection was making me laugh, and I was often happy to let him. He liked to serenade me with random songs, like Kenny Rogers's "The Gambler," and buy me silly gifts, like a giant foam finger at a Dodgers game. But while I found it endearing that he called me his Portuguese pineapple, it was harder to pretend that I wasn't bothered by his talk of the "cute little blondies" who had come into the restaurant the night before or by the fact that he wouldn't admit in front of our coworkers that he was actually into me. I could let his comments about other women go in the moment. But then, after a few drinks, when he'd get on my nerves, I'd unleash the just-beneath-the-surface stuff that had been rolling around in my brain. "Are you still talking to that actress you dated?" I asked him. "Why do you think she's so cool?" I pressed him because I wanted one certainty, one emotion out of him outside of silliness.

"God, Jessica, why do you have to ruin everything?" he huffed, which only made me want to prod him again, to get another reaction—even though I knew that reaction was never going to be "Don't worry; I'm here."

When I had to miss out on a coworker's birthday to see my mom, I hoped that it would open the door for Ben to ask me how she was doing, if I was doing OK. "It's good for you," he said with a smile, referring to my visits with my mother, a comment he also used when talking about creamed spinach or his morning wood.

Many mornings I woke up wanting to scream, my mother being the first thing I thought of. I couldn't shake the sense that she was dying, nor could I express this anxiety to Ben when I looked over and saw his blond eyelashes shut, nary a worry to disturb his dreams. By the time he woke up, I was torn between wanting to grab my clothes, get in my car, and take a long drive out to nowhere or clutching Ben's bicep and begging him to hold me. Instead, I usually putzed around on his dirty living room carpet until it seemed like I had overstayed my welcome, or he threw on a tank top, grabbed his basketball, and motioned toward the door.

During my weekly visits with my mother, whenever she'd get desperate for small talk, she'd ask me about my love life.

"It's fine, Mom," I told her one afternoon, not looking up from my *People* magazine.

"Are you still dating that stuntman?"

"Yes, Mom."

"The one with the blue eyes?"

"Yes, Mom. His eyes are still blue."

"Did you know that you have a recessive blue-eye gene on my side of the family?"

"What are you talking about?" I asked, engrossed in photos of celebrity spring flings.

"Yeah, one of my aunts had blue eyes. And you know what a recessive blue-eye gene means?"

"I'm afraid I don't wanna know."

"There's a possibility you could have blue-eyed babies."

I looked squarely at my mother. "I'm not really worried about that now, Mom."

For the first time in my dating history, my mom seemed to like my boyfriend, probably because she hadn't met him. She could imagine him to be whatever she wanted, not poor or gothy like the local ones, but some kind of haole Prince Charming. Or maybe she just needed to envision my future, one she could imagine based on the parts laid out before her.

If I wanted love advice, which was rare, I turned to Shellee. When I was dating Isaac and the two of us got into our first argument, I pulled up that familiar barstool in the kitchen, the one I sat on to watch Shellee make dinner when I was in middle school, and complained about how Isaac had blown his paycheck within the first few days of cashing it and how he'd prioritized buying a new amp for his guitar over fixing his car. She told me that sooner or later, I'd realize nothing new would ever come up in my relationships. "It'll always be the same problems, the same patterns over and over again."

When Shellee called me in LA, I didn't mention Ben. I still wasn't sure how to describe my relationship with him. I wasn't sure I wanted to think about what our pattern was. Shellee was one of the few people who'd ask how my mom was doing. In a recent phone call, Shellee had asked if we'd thought to bring anyone in, like a home health aide, for a few hours a day on a few days a week. We didn't need to do this all alone, she said. It hadn't dawned on me that we could hire a professional, that we could actually ask for help. I had mentioned it to Ed once after Shellee suggested it, and he had dismissed me, muttering something about not knowing whom to trust and insurance not paying for it.

Shellee was the only one I couldn't dismiss in an actual conversation about my mom with answers of "she's OK today" or "not so good." Shellee patiently waited for a response, then followed up with questions that only led to more questions, like a therapist or a journalist angling for the sound bite. Like someone who cared.

One Saturday night, my shift got canceled unexpectedly. I was about to head next door when Daniel showed up. He hadn't been around much since that time we made out, spending most nights at his girlfriend's to work on their relationship.

But on this spring night, he came in and declared he was thirsty. He had just finished his finals and needed to unwind. I grabbed a bottle of tequila from the kitchen cupboard, and he cut the limes. Several shots later, we wandered down to the Beauty Bar and in and out of the Burgundy

Room before stumbling into the Three Clubs. By ten to 2:00 a.m., we were at the 7-Eleven on Cahuenga, buying a six-pack of Corona to take to the Hotel Café, where we could hide the beers under the pool table in the back room and continue to drink illegally until the sun came up.

Earlier in the evening, Daniel had asked me about "the Christmas party guy," going out of his way to purposely forget Ben's name. Later, he asked me again. I evaded his questions until I could no longer count what drink or hour we were on.

"So have you slept with him?" Daniel asked.

"Jeez, Daniel." I stared at my feet, dangling from my bench near the pool table.

"Why are you so shy all of a sudden?" he asked, moving closer to me. I was wedged between his body and the pillar that propped up my head.

"Fine. We had sex," I mumbled, hoping my answer was satisfying enough for him to move on to another topic.

"Well, how was he?"

"Daniel, c'mon. Isn't it your turn to shoot?"

"You c'mon. Tell me. You always tell me."

I could have said that I actually liked Ben. I could have stood up and yelled "no" or "forget it," but it was easier to fall back into our banter. "Ben is, you know, a handsome jock type."

"What does that mean?"

"Well," I said with a shrug, "he's always been able to get by on that. He's never had to try too hard."

Daniel let out a big ah-ha laugh that immediately made me want to backpedal. "So, what you're basically saying is that he's not very good?" Daniel asked.

"I mean, he's big."

"How big?"

"Daniel, stop."

"How big?"

"Just trust me," I said, looking him in the eye. "He's big."

I excused myself to the bathroom. I was happy to return to a conversation that had shifted to the bad folk singers strumming in the corner.

Later that night, when Daniel and I got back to the apartment, I cracked open another beer. I had barely taken a sip before I fell asleep on the couch.

I woke up to Daniel carrying me up the stairs. His right arm readjusted the bend in my knees, pulling me closer to him. I remember thinking, *How kind of him to put me in bed.* Then my gaze fell back to black.

Suddenly, I was swept with a flash of panic. A jolt, like something horrible had happened to my mother or I'd left the stove on.

I wanted to open my eyes, but my eyelashes felt locked. My lids rose, shut, and rose again. The room was dark, with only a hint of silhouetted furniture against the light of a motel's neon sign across the street, blinking through my bedroom window.

Straining my neck, I made out Daniel's head of hair between my legs at the end of the bed. My comforter was underneath me, my knees were bent to the ceiling, and my underwear was wrapped around one ankle. His tongue moved rapidly, like he was mopping my insides.

I used my elbows to hoist myself up, bracing my weight on my forearms. Moving, concentrating, and speaking seemed like impossible tasks to do simultaneously.

"What the . . . what the fuck are you doing?"

His tongue left my body. He tilted his face up toward mine.

"Am I better than him?" he asked.

"Daniel, stop it." My stomach muscles caved. My elbows collapsed. My back hit the mattress with a muffled thud. Before I could form another sentence, I was out again.

A few minutes later, my eyes flashed open. Daniel's hair was flopping back and forth as he swaggered over me. His hands were on my stomach, his hips thrusting and jutting, though his body seemed too far to reach. Like I was in another room.

"What are you doing?" I moaned.

He continued to jab. Faster and faster. My mouth was dry from the heaviness of the words that wouldn't come out. I lunged toward him, droopy and startled by the weight of my head. My palms pushed into his chest.

"Get the fuck off!"

I fell back against the mattress once again. Daniel pulled himself out without finishing. I lifted my head, only managing to keep it up for a second, like a kid who could no longer tread water in the deep end. I watched him leave through the open door.

Undone

As a young adult in Los Angeles, I had plenty of outlets to preoccupy my mind: chores to do, calories to lose, my own opinions, other people's opinions, conversations I anticipated having. But some days, none of the mind tricks worked to distract me from all the feelings I was trying to avoid—they might have kept my brain busy, but they weren't coming in organized streams. They were piling up, somersaulting over each other in my mind. To alleviate them just a little, I had to busy my body, too, keep moving, even if it was just to run errands or pick up shifts at the restaurant.

I thought of my nana, in the later stages of Alzheimer's, walking from the front door to the back door, eager to get out, though she had no clue where she wanted to go or why. She'd press the button on the screen door handle several times, then turn around and make a beeline across the house to the kitchen door. She'd jangle the knob one way, then the other. Then she'd go back the same way she'd come. The mechanics of how to open a door was imprinted in her memory, but she couldn't hold on to a thought long enough to figure out why it wasn't working. She couldn't remember to check the lock. Instead, she kept repeating the same route over and over again, hoping for a different result because she didn't know what else to do.

I kept doing the things I knew, too, even if it didn't help me escape—making plans, showing up where people asked, being around anybody who wanted me there. But I also started to have a hard time managing when and how to do routine things. I had no gauge of what tasks were worth stressing over or what I needed to prioritize, so I formed a new mind trick. I started to rely on numbers or, more precisely, time, to determine how I should go about my day. I trusted randomness more than my gut. If I had a question, such as, *Should I wait until tomorrow to visit my mom?* I'd look at the last number on the clock to give me my answer. If it was even, like if the time was 1:52 or 9:04, that meant yes, I could wait another day to see her. I'd tell myself that 9:04 meant she wouldn't whimper a disappointed "oh" when I called to say I wasn't coming. Evens gave me permission to do what I wanted or what was easy. Odds bullied me into making the more excruciating decision. And in questions of fate, like, *Will the cancer spread to her brain?* odds confirmed my worst fears. But then I'd move on to what I should have for dinner or if I should call Ben because my mind was intent on avoiding any inkling of loss. My body refused to stop and fall apart.

At work, my closest friends asked me about my mom and suggested I take time off, especially as I dropped glasses with more frequency and grew impatient with customers. But I brushed them off, said I was fine. "Let's just get a drink after work," I told them, even though alcohol was now less effective at cooling my brain down.

Hanging out with Ben also wasn't the balm I wanted it to be. I didn't say anything to him about Daniel. I wasn't sure if he'd think I'd cheated on him. Often, I went over to Ben's apartment just so he would lie next to me. But to get to that point, I believed I had to have sex with him first. Our sex was no longer about adventure or me relishing my power. It was about exerting the least amount of effort I could without him noticing I wasn't really into it. When we walked through the door, I hoped he was too exhausted or drunk to instigate foreplay. Instead, I got on top for a few minutes, and then we switched, in a lazy attempt to mix it up. I didn't try to meet his eyes. I just stared into his chest, telepathically trying to make him come as quickly as possible.

The only person I told about Daniel was Mong. "Like, Daniel has a sex problem," I said, as if that was the moral of the story.

"Oh, Jes," she said, looking at me with concern. I could tell she had a better name for what had happened, but she didn't want to say it out loud, either.

"Maybe we should get our own place again," she told me, "without Daniel." I nodded. I was glad she'd suggested it. I didn't want to be the one to make it a big deal.

"It's your mom." The hostess handed me the phone. I looked at her, puzzled, as I took the receiver out of her hand one evening. I didn't know my mom had the number to my job or even remembered the name of the restaurant I worked at.

"Hello?"

"Jessica?" My mother's voice was quivering. Her Kleenex scratched the receiver.

"Why did you call me *here*?" I asked.

She told me Ed needed to go to the hospital, that he was shaking and couldn't stop.

"What do you mean, like a seizure or a nervous breakdown?"

"I don't know, not a seizure," she said. He was leaving, so I needed to come over right then.

"Mom, I'm working. I'm in charge," I said, sighing into the phone. I had just become an assistant manager, which meant I ran the restaurant on Sundays when no one else wanted to work. "Can't this wait until tomorrow?"

"I think he really has to leave."

"Ughhh, Mom." I sighed. "I gotta call my boss, see if she can come down. I gotta set up these reservations. I mean, we're in the middle of the dinner rush." My mother was quiet. I could tell she wasn't going to give up. "Huhhhh. OK. Fine. Let me get off the phone and figure this out."

I knew that a good daughter, a daughter who understood her kuleana, would say, "Screw this crappy job, let the restaurant fend for itself!" and run to tend to her mother. But even after my boss told me she completely understood and would come down to relieve me, I waited until she got there to order dinner, then took my time packing up my eggplant parmesan before heading over to the gas station to buy a pack of cigarettes and make the ninety-mile drive to Temecula.

When I arrived at their house that evening, Ed was already back from the hospital. They were sitting at the kitchen table and told me to grab a seat. When I asked what happened, Ed said it had something to do with his sinuses, with him being dehydrated, but the doctors had told him to head home. It was clear that more than being ill, he was exhausted, frustrated, and angry. He stood up, jabbed a finger at me, and said I needed to help out more. Once a week wasn't enough.

"But I work five, sometimes six nights a week," I told him. "I can't afford to scale back."

"At least one more day a week," he insisted.

I looked over at my mother across from me. She gave me that "behave" look that she had used when I was a kid whining for a toy in the store.

"Sure, yeah," I told Ed, gazing past their heads at the beaded lamp they had bought to decorate their new start.

That night, I took my mother back to her bed and lay with her for a few hours before she started to doze. Next to her, my stomach rumbled, and I remembered the giant piece of eggplant I'd eaten. *How much cardio will I have to do tomorrow to get rid of that?* I looked at the clock—2:37, an odd, uncomfortable number.

With my mother's eyes shut, the hum of her breathing deep and steady, I scooted off the edge of the bed and closed the door to her bathroom behind me. I began rummaging through her medicine cabinet. Excedrin, Tylenol, an old comb. Under her sink stood a big bottle of Tums and a box of ex-lax. I popped one, two, three, four round *e*'s out of their silver wrapper and put them into my mouth, washing them down with a handful of water from the sink. I put four more in my pocket for later.

The next morning, I was planning my escape over coffee when Ed told me I needed to stay and watch my mother. I told him I had errands to run; I needed to get my oil changed. Ed slammed his hand on the counter. "Leave now, then! You know what, just never come back!"

I picked up my keys and was about to head toward the door, but then something snapped. Ed had already walked out of the kitchen, but I was right behind him, my breath on his neck. I started yelling. "You need to suck it up and get help! You've gone over the fucking edge! You're fucking losing it!"

As I followed Ed around the condo, I told him he needed to check his ego. That because he was unable to ask for help, he had to demand it from me.

"Where did you learn to be such an ugly, unmannered young woman?" he asked.

Suddenly, my mom appeared in the doorway of her bedroom, looking out into the hallway at us, bracing herself unsteadily. I had not seen her get out of bed on her own since she moved to California. "Stop, Jessica, stop! What are you doing?" she called out. Ed stormed off into the spare room, slamming the door. "You can't talk to Ed like that," she kept on. "You said the ego thing too harshly." I looked at her, slumped against the doorframe, her hand trembling to keep herself upright. I hated her. I loved her. I grabbed her around the shoulders and walked her back to bed.

Less than two weeks later, Ed put my mother in a nursing home. My mom called me, hysterical. She thought Ed was taking her for a doctor's visit, and the next thing she knew, she was being wheeled past men and women much older than her down hallways that smelled of microwaved vegetables and vapor rub. "You have to get me out of here!" I told her I'd come up with a plan and give her a call back.

I decided not to phone Ed. He hadn't informed me about the nursing home. My mom was turning to me, not him. Finally, I had a purpose, a concrete decision to make, an opportunity to be the one to save her.

However, I didn't know where to begin. Would I go there and rescue her from the nursing home? Would I ask Mong to help me? I imagined bumping into Ed in the hallway, explaining to him why I was suddenly taking charge. I'd have to hoist my limp, heavy mother up into my SUV, keep her comfortable in a seat that barely reclined, set her up in some square of our apartment not covered in random messes, and then divvy up the precise medications for her on the hour. For the first time, I wanted to learn what it took, what I was signing up for.

I racked my brain for all the doctors' names she'd mentioned and scoured the internet for them in any facility near Temecula. In the seven years my mom had lupus and the two she had breast cancer, I never once went with her to a doctor's visit. I only asked the doctors condescending questions when they appeared in her hospital room during her stays for emergency treatment or surgeries.

When I finally reached her oncologist, the woman told me that it was she who had persuaded Ed to put my mother in a nursing home. She needed around-the-clock care, the doctor told me, care that Ed and I couldn't provide. "She's pretty far gone," the doctor said.

I didn't ask how far; I didn't dwell on the fact that things had gotten so bad that an outsider had to step in and reassess the situation for us.

Before I could ask any more questions, the doctor said that my mother had already checked herself out of the home.

"What? How can a woman who can't get out of bed just walk out the door?"

The oncologist said Ed had come and picked her up. "Your mother was giving everyone a hard time. She wouldn't stop asking why Ed had left her," she told me.

I was at the gym one day when I started to have a panic attack. I called one of my hiking friends, Claire, who invited me over to her apartment. She handed me a beer and listened as I told her that I didn't know what was wrong with me. I was losing my mind. Claire made a bold suggestion: write it all down. Writing could offer clarity, a way to organize my thoughts, or at the very least, a lifeline of release. Wasn't I a writer, after all?

When the Hawaiian monarchy was overthrown just before the turn of the twentieth century, writing down mo'olelo became urgent for the Kānaka to preserve a culture under siege. Mo'olelo was necessary for recording not only banned practices, like the hula, but also other ways of life, such as food preparation and recreation, like surfing. There are stories of Hi'iaka dominating ali'i surfers who were rude or overconfident, but she also helped them heal through the sport, a counternarrative to the modern imagery of surfing as a bro-ish activity. In other mo'olelo, Pele and Hi'iaka traverse the 'āina, visiting kalo farmers and women who pick limu. The sisters are treated with respect as they feast with maka'āinana and put bossy ali'i in their place.

Some of these mo'olelo were published in Hawaiian nativist papers; a few made their way to English-language ones. Over the years, haole scholars have collected and sold these tales as myths, told through their own perceptions and cultural interpretations, not through the lens of those who actually lived mana wahine or aloha 'āina. As ho'omanawanui points out in *Voices of Fire*, in the haole's telling, male surfers are transformed into the protagonists, and the sport is an individual one "reserved for kings." There's no mention of the communal and spiritual practice of surfing. Any reader who picks up the popular *Hawaiian Mythology* by Martha Beckwith or a brochure titled "Hawaiian Legends" might read the stories of Pele and her sisters as cutesy fables about women creating chaos or a scorned volcano lady, but when Kānaka wrote down and published their moʻolelo, it was not to provide tales for mass entertainment or fodder for trolley tours. It was to sustain their cultural practices and push back on how colonial society saw them: wāhine were not sweet Natives to ogle or possess as treasures, but athletes, competitors, warriors.

In history lessons, the Kānaka, and other indigenous people across the globe, are often portrayed as victims without agency, or they're erased completely. But they have always been there, fighting back, trying to keep their culture alive. Their survival is perhaps the ultimate moʻolelo: darkness will come, but to endure, you have to hold on to whatever light you can.

One afternoon, a few days after Claire said to write it all down, I sat at my desk. I opened my journal that had sat untouched for weeks and wrote, *Why* . . . I let my pen linger there in the empty space for a few seconds before my mind started to hopscotch over itself. I began making deep, dark scribble-scrabbles across the page. It felt good to press down hard, to watch the ink spread out toward the edges, to make a mess. Then I closed the journal. I wasn't ready to explore my own story. I didn't have it in me to keep this moment alive.

Even moʻolelo about Pele and men are often still stories of mana wahine. Probably the best known are those that tell of Pele and Kamapuaʻa, a half man and half hog, as both bitter rivals and lovers. In one, he arrives on the Big Island as a handsome man from Oʻahu to seduce Pele. Her sisters point him out to her, but Pele is not interested, calling him a pig. She summons her akua to stoke the fire in Halemaʻumaʻu Crater. Lava erupts, rolling down the volcano until it reaches Kamapuaʻa's feet. Furious, the pig-man turns around and summons his own god to smolder Pele's fire; his sister, who's part rain cloud, follows, extinguishing the rest of Pele's flames. Pele and Kamapuaʻa go back and forth like this, destroying each other's homes and families, then leaving time for regrowth and refueling, before doing it all over again. The chasing is constant, the anger endless. They almost come to a truce—she seems to even give in to his advances—until he takes more than she is willing to give and rapes her. In this telling, Kapo, another one of Pele's sisters and the goddess of fertility, throws her vagina at Kamapuaʻa so that he will leave Pele alone. It works; Kamapuaʻa runs after it, chasing her kohe from island to island, until it leaves a crater on Oʻahu's south shore.

It is easy to read this moʻolelo and get caught up in the salacious push and pull of their relationship, to recognize that even the most powerful female entity is no match for male violence. But the more compelling takeaway is about the strength of mana wahine. Terrible things are going to happen, horrible moments that will cause loss and suffering and shame, and there is nothing you can do to stop them. But what you can do is reach out when things go wrong, lean on each other, help how you can.

Sometimes I think that my mother and I did all that we knew how to do for each other. Many other times, I wish, just for a few moments, that we were able to open up about our own narratives and let one another into our pain. What if she had abandoned the "everything's fine" pleasantries and told me about the child she had given up for adoption or showed me her anger and sadness over my father leaving? Would I have been comfortable telling her about my DUI, my rape, my fear of living without her? What if I had opened up to her about my own pregnancy scares and self-doubts? Would she have seen there was nothing to be ashamed of? Could we have eventually looked past our individual hurt to make space for the other's?

The second and final time Ed put my mother in a nursing home, I did try to reach out to her. But I didn't make it about her fears; I made it about mine.

I walked into her room at the facility, sat in the chair next to her bed, and started to cry. I told her I was scared. How the thought of never touching her gray curls again made me want to cut off a lock and stick it in my purse pocket, how the idea of never hearing her sweet, feminine voice again made me want to take it from her throat and keep it in my hands.

She refused to turn toward me. Her head sunk deeper into her pillow. I went on, asking her if she remembered how she felt when her own mother was dying of cancer. I reminded her that I didn't have a husband or a child of my own, nor brothers or sisters from her. I had no one to gauge how I was supposed to react to the end of my mother's life.

Her eyes suddenly looked heavier, surely encouraged by an onslaught of medication. I reached over to shake her shoulder, lightly, just enough to get her attention. Then I asked her how long she thought she had left. What she really felt. "Shouldn't you know best?" I asked. I needed to know how long I would have to endure the anxiety of waiting and seeing her like this.

I would've sat there for as long as it took for her to give me an honest answer. A few minutes later, she responded. "A year, maybe two." Her tone was cheery and light, as if I'd asked her when she had planned to take an Alaskan cruise.

Three weeks later, she died.

"Don't tell her" was the last complete sentence I ever heard my mom say. Ed and I were standing beside her bed, and she was looking at him.

"Don't tell her," she said again, her eyes wide and intense, her back struggling to lift from the mattress, until a nurse came in to sedate her. I knew the "her" was me, but at the time, I dismissed the entire episode as delusion or medicated nonsense, my mother fighting to hold on to her mind.

I wouldn't find out about my mom giving up a kid for adoption until a year later, when I saw Ed for the last time. He had asked me to lunch, and over sandwiches at a Denny's in Temecula, he told me he didn't want to be burdened with this secret any longer. She never wanted me to know, he said. When I asked why, he told me, "She was ashamed."

In stories I've read of other women who were sent to maternity homes prior to *Roe*, giving up a child was the most defining event of their lives, even if they went on to have families and careers. One woman said she met birth mothers in her support group who went on to die from cancers in their fifties. My mother may have been technically dying from diagnosable diseases, but shame had taken its toll, too. It gripped her up until her very last words.

If you asked me in the middle of a night at the Beauty Bar, when I was high on vodka and a new pair of hip-hugging jeans, if I was shameful, I would have scoffed at you. I was someone who did what she wanted, who said what she wanted. I was fearless, like my dad had declared. But shame functions as a wall: on one side, the presentation of self for others to see; on the other, the parts you tell yourself you need to hide—the failed writer, the drunk woman assaulted by a man she trusted, the moron who couldn't live and be happy in the most beautiful place on Earth, the selfish daughter who was angry at her dying mother for having to take care of her. I hated that every other young person I knew seemed to be having the time of their lives while I had to listen to my mother's shallow breath, and then I felt ashamed for having those feelings and not just sucking it up and patiently sitting by her side. It seemed ridiculous and impossible to keep pretending to be some kind of tough, good-times hula girl in combat boots who let everything slide off her.

When my mother's body started shutting down and hospice gave her four days to live, I felt a glimmer of relief. Here was a concrete schedule—four days, an even number! I could let my job and friends and family know. I could maybe even be present in these last moments of her life. But what was in front of me became excruciating to watch. She had become mostly incoherent, often passed out from the morphine, but she did not necessarily seem peaceful. Her pattern of startled snores did not give the impression that she was ready to ease out of this life.

It was then, her organs struggling, her mind drifting in and out of consciousness, that I decided she should finally meet Ben.

Even though I planned for their introduction on a day Ben and I normally didn't work, he put me off. He was maybe going for a bike ride with his friends and had to go with his roommate to check out a location for a shoot. I ignored him. I told him snippets of what the doctors had said, how my mom was pretty heavily medicated. I fluctuated between a very matter-of-fact tone and my voice cracking in hysteria. I wasn't sure which reaction would get him to come down to Temecula.

After hemming and hawing, he agreed to make the ninety-mile drive to "stop by."

I met Ben outside of the automatic doors, greeting him with a hug as if he'd arrived for brunch, walking him past the clinical check-in desk, down the bare white halls, and into my mom's sterile, undecorated room. "Mom, this is Ben," I said, reaching out for his arm behind me. She was sitting up in a loose hospital gown, untied in the back. Her head was wobbly with morphine.

As I pulled Ben out from behind me—surprise!—she let out a few peeps, her eyes widening, sensing that this man meant something to me.

Unsure of what to do, Ben extended his hand toward hers. She cooed at him, then at me, and I stood there and watched him fumble as he put his hand back into his pocket. Within a few minutes, she was asleep.

I pulled up an extra chair on my side of the bed for Ben. I told him about how she had eaten a whole donut that morning. "Um, that's great," he said. He scanned the plastic tray on her nightstand, the window shade lifted halfway, and the bumps on the ceiling before settling his focus on the television suspended in the far corner. Just like at home, the television at the nursing home was always on at a low hum.

From the corner of my eye, I saw Ben fidget in his chair and couldn't help but feel a little smug at his discomfort. *This is how it feels to me every day, motherfucker.* I leaned back in my chair and crossed my feet in front of me, showing him that this was my life—would he care to get comfortable?

After twenty minutes, he said he had to go.

My head snapped toward him. "I knew you'd been dying to leave since you got here!" I flung my arm in the air. "I knew it!"

My mother was undisturbed by my outburst. Ben shook his head and got up.

I followed him into the hallway, berating him with questions about what big plans he had to tend to. He mentioned something about meeting up with friends and the actress he once dated. I told him to go be with her already. She was fun. They could have fun together. I followed him out of the automatic doors and into the parking lot.

Ben finally turned around to yell back, confirming that, yes, what we were doing was not his idea of a good time. "Don't be so insecure," he said.

He started walking toward his car. I yelled at him that he was being a dick. The farther he got away, the louder I yelled, "Fuck you." Once he was in his car, I screamed, "My mom is dying, you asshole!" But I knew he could not hear me.

My anger was not like Pele's. Hers was direct, just. Mine was indirect, hitting the wrong targets over low stakes. The end was near, and I was still afraid to really let go, to unleash the fire of my true emotions.

Ed was not faring much better than I was. By day two, neither of us could sit next to my mother for more than several minutes at a time. And it was even harder for us to be there together, our grief mirrored in each other's faces. Ed was many things, but he loved my mother, and seeing her so diminished tore him apart.

By day three, Ed and I had stopped seeing each other around the facility, and I started driving back to my apartment every night. Mong came down with me one afternoon and sat beside my mom and prayed because she didn't know what else to do. My best friend from high school, Melanie, drove down from San Francisco for a few hours just to say goodbye, too. Since this was several years before texting, I received numerous voice mails of "I'm so sorry" from coworkers who knew why I had taken off work for an indefinite amount of time.

But then my mom kept living past those four days that hospice had forecasted. It became impossible to be at the nursing home at all, watching a desperate woman fight against her body shutting down. That's when I did it. I called my dad.

Even as I waited for my father to answer his phone, I didn't want to ask him to fly up from Hawai'i. I hoped he'd just offer. "My mom's still hanging in there, but I don't know how much longer I can," I told him. He said he could come up in a few days, but one day was all he could take off work. "Oh, sure," I said, hoping my mother wouldn't live past that one day he was in town.

A few hours later, my dad called back. "Shellee will come after I leave," he said. I felt my grip on the phone relax, letting it rest close to my neck. I knew my dad wouldn't leave me hanging, even if he wasn't able to be there himself.

When I picked up my dad from the airport, I asked him if it was OK if we didn't go back to the nursing home right away to see the vegetable of a woman he was once married to. "Sure," he said, shrugging his shoulders. He knew nothing about Temecula, but he knew there had to be a mall nearby.

"Are you hungry?" he asked when we arrived at the Promenade.

"Not really."

He spotted an ice cream stand in the corner. "How 'bout some ice cream? I could go fo' a shake."

I shrugged. "OK."

I poked my spoon around my cup of ice cream, picking out the chunks of cookie dough as we circled all the shops. The smell of Cinnabon and freshly baked pretzels made me nauseous, and I tossed my cup into a garbage can. School had just gotten out, and a barrage of preteens charged past us, most of them competing to talk over each other. Kiosk workers popped up in our pathway. "I think you'd look great with straight hair," a woman holding a flat iron suggested as we passed her stand. From behind another kiosk, a man jumped out, promising us a deal on a cell phone. Every gesture seemed crass; every word rang in my ears. Little interruptions no longer brushed past me; they felt like tiny needles pricking my skin.

I followed my dad in and out of stores. I even tried on a few shirts and a pair of sunglasses just to keep myself busy.

"You need anyting? A jacket? It's getting cold," my dad asked as we got on the escalator.

"No," I said, keeping my head down. The black metal lines across the steps of the escalator looked sharp. I had an urge to rub my face against them. "What was Mom like when you were dating?" I asked as we got off on the second floor.

"Huh? I dunno, girlie." He reached back to put his arm around me. "Dat was a long time ago."

I glanced up at my father, hoping he'd recall something, some small detail. "What did you like about my mom?" I tried again.

He thought for a moment as we walked into the leather goods store. He paused. "She was always happy-go-lucky. I liked dat about her."

Around midafternoon, he suggested we finally go see my mother. "Here, I'll drive," he said, his open palm summoning my car keys. I slumped into the passenger seat, relieved that he was taking control.

Two minutes later, he made a left turn into a gas station. Without a word, he opened the door and jumped out. I knew he was just getting fuel, just taking care of business, but I twisted in my seat, craning my head to keep him in eyesight. I could see his waist, his hand gripped securely around the gas pump. Knowing he was close wasn't enough. I had to be closer. I got out of the car.

"So what do you have to do at home tomorrow, Dad? Why do you have to leave?"

He mumbled something about a bid for a job. "Did you talk to Shellee?" he asked, clicking the pump for the last drip of gas. "I think she comes in around lunchtime."

As promised, Shellee arrived at the nursing home before noon the day after my father left. She stayed for five nights, right up until the hours before my mother passed away. Even though Shellee's presence was softer, her face less expectant than my dad's, I grew more antsy sitting in my mother's room when she was there. She looked at my mother with empathy; she could, and would, rub lotion on the arm of this woman she barely knew, the woman who was once married to her husband and probably hated her. I had to walk out of the room, unable to even bargain with myself to sit still through another commercial break. Ed must've felt the same way. I never saw him around the nursing home anymore.

Shellee detected this churning inside of me, so she found us places to walk to and drives to go on. We often went in search of something to eat. She told me how she'd spent days with her mom in bed before she, too, had died of cancer. They'd laughed like never before, stuffing their faces with the See's Candies her mother had stashed under her bed. Shellee had managed to enjoy those moments with her mom. I wanted nothing more than to be that present. I also wanted this to all be over.

No one was there when my mom died.

As I was driving Shellee to the airport, a nurse called to say that she had walked in to check on my mom and found she wasn't breathing. She went peacefully, the nurse assured me.

When I walked into my mother's room again, Ed was sitting there, crying. Her body was still in bed, propped up in a seated position, her head slightly tilted toward the ceiling. Her mouth hung wide open, as if letting out one final scream. All I could think was, *Why didn't the nurse close her lips?* Why couldn't she follow through on her clichéd sentiment and let me believe my mother had indeed died peacefully?

I started to wail, or what my ancestors call *kūmākena*, along with Ed. I touched my mother's cold body because I thought that was what I should do. That's when I noticed the Hawaiian ring I'd given to her eight years ago for her fiftieth birthday was on her finger. She had never owned any fancy jewelry, and since I couldn't afford a diamond, I thought I'd get her the next best thing. Hawaiian heirloom jewelry, often gold with black enamel lettering over subtle etchings of plumeria and hibiscus, is usually gifted by a loved one on a special occasion; my parents had bought me a bracelet with my name translated into Hawaiian, Eikika, for my thirteenth birthday. The ring I'd chosen for my mom said "Sarah." Inside, I'd inscribed "Love Jes '94," like I was signing her yearbook. I picked up her clammy hand and slipped the ring off and into my pocket.

A nurse came in and asked us if we wanted a few more minutes with her before the coroner took her away. Ed and I shook our heads and stood to leave. As soon as we turned the corner out of the room, toward the exit, our kūmākena ceased.

Returning Home

Hours after my mom died, I booked a ticket to Hawaiʻi. Home is where I wanted to go.

I had been back several times in the two years since I'd moved away, but this time my childhood bedroom seemed especially unfamiliar. My bloodred comforter had been replaced with a pastel quilt Shellee had made; my Cure posters had been taken down, leaving the walls bare. While it was nice to have the entire downstairs to myself in college, having taken it over after Uncle Mano died, now the bottom floor seemed desolate while the rest of my family was upstairs.

My dad carried my suitcase to my room, then opened his arms for a hug. I leaned in, burying my head in his chest. I didn't want to let go because I knew as soon as I did, he'd leave the room. Sure enough, he patted me on the back and headed upstairs.

"Hey, Dad, what are you doing later?" I called from the doorway.

"How 'bout sushi for dinner?" he asked.

"Yeah, OK, sure," I mumbled. But I didn't need a question. I needed a plan. I wanted him to tell me what to do and when to do it.

I zeroed in on the alarm clock's neon numbers: 1:10. Six hours to go if we had an early dinner. How could I fill up every second of those six hours? I calculated the number of minutes I needed to take a shower (twenty if I drew a bath); to blow-dry my hair (fifteen if I straightened it, too); to pace around the room until I headed upstairs (five), waited on the couch (ten), and tried not to look desperate (impossible).

My fixation with time continued. My mother was already dead, and I was still parsing minutes, measuring hours. I didn't know what else I was waiting for.

Once I settled in, mornings in Hawai'i seemed longer even than those evenings in Temecula. On day two, I scurried upstairs to find open cereal boxes littering the counter and Marshal's forgotten textbook on the kitchen table. I opened the screen door to peek at the carport. My dad's truck was gone. But Shellee's car was still there.

I knocked on her bedroom door, hoping Shellee had nothing and everything to do, and maybe I could tag along? She said she was going to the grocery store. "We could buy some stuff to make brownies later," she said, her palm guiding the back of my shoulder as we crossed the doorway. After the store, I went with her to the dog groomers, the gas station, and the post office. In the next few days, I offered to take my papa to get a haircut and to drop off Marshal at the mall. I was even happy when Shellee made me a dentist appointment—another two hours I didn't have to plan myself. My ancestors had a word for this, too—*naʻauʻauā hele*—to be so grief stricken, you wander endlessly. But back then, I just thought my inclinations were an abnormality.

Things were easier after nightfall, when I was physically exhausted from the circus in my mind. Often, I made plans with friends. I hoped to find the old Jessica at the bar, the one who could have fun and laugh, a fresh coat of vodka giving her brain a break. But it wasn't like I was there on vacation. Everyone I had dinner and drinks with knew why I was back. While I had no problem relaying the logistical details about the end of my mother's life or talking shit about Ed, I didn't know what to say beyond that. It was hard watching my friends' reactions, seeing their concerned faces, hearing their condolences of "I'm sorry" and the lingering silence afterward. None of them had yet lost a parent; no one understood what it was like to watch their mother die. This dance of all of us trying to put each other and ourselves at ease only made me feel more separate from them.

There were moments when I just wanted to get drunk. To go to the old dive that my coworkers and I used to hit up after the club and let the jukebox drown out any chance of a conversation. But that's not what happened. Instead of blurring into the scene, I traced my finger around the rim of my glass, fiddled with my straw. I kicked my slippers on and off, nodding at jokes, taking the cues from my friends' smiles to return one of my own.

"Hey, Jessica, remember the time when . . ."

"Yeah, sure," I said, only hearing the first line of my friend's story before I jumped out of my chair. I needed to get up. I needed to go to the bathroom. I pushed the door open and braced myself against the sink. In the mirror, I watched my face crinkle and crinkle into a silent shout. Or did I want to cry? I walked into the stall and sat on the toilet with my head in my hands. Until I couldn't sit there anymore, either.

Unable to be the party girl my friends once knew, I started spending more nights at home. Knocking on my dad and Shellee's door had become an evening habit as well. "What are you guys watching?" I asked, peeking my head in. *The Sopranos*, *Independence Day*, old black-and-white movies—it didn't matter. I crawled into their bed and sandwiched myself between them. I didn't follow the plot and sometimes didn't bother to laugh. I just lay there. When I heard the unharmonious drone of their snores, I scooted off their mattress and walked back downstairs into the dark.

But there was a purpose for this trip home: to plan my mother's funeral.

Much like with a child's placenta, Kānaka, particularly makaʻāinana, often buried members of their ʻohana close to their home. They believe a person holds mana in their bones, and it's important to put their mana back into the ground where your family lives. The living coinciding with the dead, loved ones always with you.

But Ed did not want to bury my mom in Hawaiʻi or scatter her ashes in Waiʻanae like she had joked. He had her cremated but wouldn't say exactly what he planned to do with her box of dust afterward. He did, though, agree that it made sense to hold her funeral where she had lived for most of her life. So he handed me her address book and told me to plan it.

I'm not sure what kind of funeral my mother would have wanted. She'd probably decide to have it at the Episcopalian church where she and Ed were married because that's what Ed would want her to do, and this I know because Ed himself told me to hold it there. But if it was up to her, would she rather have a casual gathering on the beach or in the quad outside her classroom in Waiʻanae? Perhaps not; she hated being in the sun too long. Would she have wanted to bypass the ceremony and just gather at the tavern where she drank with her coworkers on Friday evenings? Or had that been their bar of choice, not hers? How about Monterey Bay Canners, where she often took me? Or did we go there all the time because she knew I liked the stuffed mushrooms? I could see her happy with something simple and tasteful, with waiters passing crab cakes and lemon drops. Some sort of simple color theme, much like the way she decorated her Christmas tree in crystal snowflakes and strung pearls. But I couldn't bring myself to contemplate or execute any of those ideas. I couldn't remember who my mother was before she was sick.

Even though I was once someone good at executing tasks, those days, I was useless. I had to be asked by Shellee if I had planned for food or flowers. She chauffeured me around, running through our list of funeral-planning errands in a single day: to Walmart for a guest book; to a florist who specialized in both wreaths and lei making; to the neighborhood deli for aluminum trays of fried noodles and wontons, greasy pūpū eaten with chopsticks that my mom didn't even like. I'm not even sure my mom knew how to work a pair of chopsticks. I didn't care. Shellee suggested places, trying to make the process as painless for me as possible, and I went along.

The day of the funeral, I don't even remember showing up. I just remember the drone of a hundred strangers—mostly my mom's former colleagues and students, along with a handful of my high school and college friends—making small talk in the pews around me. I sat with my dad, Shellee, and brothers on one side; Ed sat with his grown children and their kids on the other, our two families divided like bridal parties at a wedding.

The preacher who had married my mother and Ed, a man who resembled Santa Claus in an aloha shirt, walked to the pulpit and spoke of the path to righteousness and how my mother, a kind and generous woman, had surely found such a path.

I leaned forward, trying to recall the last time my mother spoke of god or faith. Certainly, she hadn't stepped foot in this church since she became ill. I thought about her holding on for three weeks, breathing erratically; sitting up, half-conscious; fighting to say something to the very end. She was not at ease with death. She had certainly not walked eagerly into the afterlife.

"Love filled the room," the preacher said. I thought of love in its idealized form—accepting, patient—and it didn't register with the anger, resentment, and guilt I was failing to tamp down. I had written and printed the funeral program, including a bio that spoke of my mother's kindness and dedication, but that was where opening my heart had ended.

Because Ed and I weren't up to the task, her best friend and Wai'anae colleague gave the eulogy. "She didn't teach English; she taught kids,"

Steve said. He told stories of how my mother was a mom to her male students and a confidante to the girls. How students would visit her years after graduating, and she'd remember something they had written in a paper or something they did at homecoming, and their faces would light up. How when another teacher would mention a student's name in the workroom, she'd say, "Oh, I love him," or "She's terrific." My mother always saw the good in people.

He also spoke of how she was the life of the party, the one who rallied people to get drinks after work, who was the last to leave. How they looked forward to making jokes and smoking cigarettes in the workroom every day. Everyone loved talking to Sarah. She put others in a good mood.

I wanted to live in Steve's speech, this place where my mother was not dying and desperate like she had been for the past seven years. How lucky most of these people were not to have seen her stuck in bed, needing to pee every twenty minutes. It made me wonder if she had not had lupus and cancer and klutziness, could we have grabbed beers together and had conversations that weren't stilted? But I was not a coworker she bantered with, nor the man from whom she sought companionship. I was her daughter, made in her image. She wanted to protect me from what she had been through, and she thought she had to hide herself to do it.

Once the service was over, Ed and I stood at the altar in front of our respective wreaths—one a tropical splash of red anthuriums and birds of paradise with a sash that read "Mother," the other springy with pom-poms of carnations with a sash that read "Wife." A stream of loved ones and strangers hugged and kissed me on the cheek as I stared right past their heads.

But still, it wasn't over. Next was the reception. My dad and Shellee positioned themselves behind the food, serving noodles and inari sushi to people who had known my mother long enough to realize that this was her cheating ex and the woman he'd left her for. Part of me wanted to join them, just so I didn't have to make small talk with my friends and near strangers. "No worries, girlie—we got it covered," my dad said.

As I was in line for food, one of my mother's former students came up from behind me. She reached inside the top of my shirt and whispered in my ear that my tag was sticking out. "Thanks," I said. "You know your mom wouldn't want you walking around like that," she said with a laugh. Her friend beside her joined in. Yes, I got it—my mom never made a fashion faux pas. But I couldn't return a smile. The nagging perfectionist was not the version of my mother I cared to remember.

Once the crowd filtered out, a woman, tall and fluid, with hair down to her waist, like an angel or Karen Carpenter, approached me in the corner where I was hiding. "Jessica, is it?" she said softly, leaning in to find my eyes, which were buried in my plate.

"Yes," I said, looking up. The sun was lowering behind her. The frizz of her hair was a warm orangey red.

She told me that she was in one of my mother's first classes at Wai'anae and that when she read the obituary in the local paper, she was shocked. How could such a vibrant woman be gone?

She reached in her purse and pulled out a cigarette, as though lighting up on church property was the most natural thing to do. I watched the smoke drift from her ash into the pinkish sky. She didn't say much else, and neither did I. When she was done, she touched my shoulder and walked away.

I opened many cards that spoke of condolences in the same but different ways. "She is in a better place now." "God is watching over her." I wished that envisioning my mother in heaven could patch up the emptiness that throbbed from the pit of my stomach. I wished that handing over my burdens to someone else—a god, a priest, a stranger who "got it"—would be the beginning and the end of the work. I wished I could blindly believe in something, even if it didn't resonate, just to feel better by the weight of one less anxiety.

But the spirituality I knew best, the beliefs I'd been fed in my Christian schooling, did not work for me. The Bible stories my elementary teachers recited sounded like tales, not truths. Not that they needed to feel real for me to believe, but rarely did they capture my imagination, either. The language was stilted; there was nothing that appealed to my reality or interests. The flood enrapturing the earth, Noah gathering the animals two by two, all that was pretty cool, and Jesus rising from the dead was a good plot twist, but many stories just seemed to center on white men in cloaks (or so the illustrations in my Bible were drawn) screwing each other over and getting tasks done. There were so many men and so few women, unless they were helpers or heathens. The woman with the greatest starring role was the one who miraculously birthed Jesus without having to taint herself with sex.

But what Christianity did provide, and what stuck with me, was a set of rules: do not steal, do not dishonor your parents, do not take another man's wife. And I believe it is those rules that continue to draw people into the church. We want to be given guidance, some kind of reassurance that if we do these things, then we will be seen as good people and rewarded with a glorious afterlife, instead of suffering and uncertainty.

In Hawai'i, Christianity did not strike just once, far and wide, when the missionaries arrived—the word of Jesus continues to grow. I had friends in high school who were raised Buddhist but were drawn to Evangelical churches with large youth groups because they wanted to be part of something, family members who converted to Christianity during times of marital strife and others who did so when they had kids because it provided a sense of structure. We are all looking for some order. It's hard to trust that light will arise from the darkness.

I'm not sure many locals give much thought as to why we aren't gathering en masse at heiau or ceremonies like the Makahiki instead. Or why many of my friends whose parents were Buddhist didn't gravitate to Buddha's teachings of mindfulness over the moral codes that are the Ten Commandments. Or why, at the very least, many of us didn't acknowledge the sun, stars, and sea in a daily moment of thanks. The natural elements are not abstract rules; they are right there within our reach.

There are numerous Hawaiian and local ministers who incorporate the Hawaiian language into Christian teachings, who revere nature and hold sermons outdoors, and some who even include lāʻau lapaʻau, or herbal healing, into their practice. Like with race and ethnicity, religion in Hawaiʻi is more blended than most. Still, a lot of the spirituality at the core of our culture continues, slowly, to be erased. The sacred sites where our ancestors are buried get built over for giant telescopes. Land that is designated for Kānaka is sold to Mark Zuckerberg to build an estate the size of two Central Parks. The ocean is harder to get to with a growing fortress of hotels surrounding the coastline. Many of my local friends—college educated, in hospitality and frontline-worker jobs—rent their homes and apartments from people who don't live in Hawaiʻi full-time. Nearly 250 years after Captain Cook first arrived in Hawaiʻi, more than 125 years after the overthrow of Queen Liliʻuokalani, capitalistic and government forces haven't stopped trying to sever both locals' and the Kānaka's access to the ʻāina, prioritizing foreign needs first.

While I was home after my mother's death, I met a college friend at Borders, across the street from Ala Moana Beach Park. The park was built on land that was once part of the Hawaiian Kingdom but was transferred to the US government after annexation; the dredging of its reefs put money in the pockets of an industrial titan while giving his wife a beautification project to chair. As my friend and I looked out over the park, surrounded by stacks of the latest Tom Clancy bestseller and the stale smell of Starbucks, I told her I just wanted to feel normal again, not so separate from the rest of the world. She was a friend who had dealt with some anxiety, too; who had a sickly father, a missing mother; who maybe saw me and wondered if this was her future. She admitted to feeling the same way at times, alone and adrift. But she said when she repeated these words at a party once, a friend had disagreed with her. "Sometimes I just stand still, look around, and I feel connected to everything," her friend said.

This idea was both familiar and abstract to me. I understood that connection was the Hawaiian way—that even in the midst of the hustle and bustle, it was still possible to marvel at the cliffs behind a brand-new shopping center, to follow the motion of the wind while standing in a parking lot. But my life had been ruled by disconnection: playing pretend, leaving for my father's house, taking off for California, dulling my mind with alcohol. It was the first step toward stillness that had always been an enigma to me: How does one stop the replayed scenarios, the imaginary conversations, the numbers games, and sit in the discomfort, instead of immediately looking for another direction to run?

Smoke Rising from the Water

A few days before I was to fly back to LA, Shellee asked me if I wanted to stay longer. I told her I couldn't. I had a job and rent and a boyfriend I'd barely talked to in weeks.

"Well, maybe you can take some time to get away," she said.

"I am away."

"I mean, really away. Where you can relax."

"Like where?" I could not fathom taking a spa vacation right then.

"Maybe somewhere you don't know anyone, and you can, you know, just chill. Go on walks, take long baths, write."

I looked at her like she had just suggested I go relive my mom's last days again. I kept my ticket and got on a plane to LA.

Within my first two weeks back, I caused a minor car accident. I burned my arm on the same pan several times, getting multiple second-degree burns from my elbow to my wrist. I took a Xanax, then drank three vodka sodas and tripped over a curb, falling hard on my face, scraping my entire left cheek and cracking my front tooth. At work, my patience with customers wore so thin I started rolling my eyes at tables before even turning away. I took deep breaths before I walked in the door every evening to prepare myself for the dinner rush. In between orders, I ran to the bathroom to wash my hands, a trick a coworker taught me to get rid of the "negative energy" I was holding on to. Sometimes I would just sit on the toilet, fully clothed, and press my palms into my eye sockets.

Then Shellee called. My dad was cheating on her.

In fact, he had been cheating on her while Shellee was comforting me in Temecula. After he'd sat with me at his ex-wife's bedside, he got back on a plane to see this other woman, sending his current wife in his place to comfort me. Two birds, one stone.

"What the fuck do you think you're doing?" I screamed into the phone at my dad. "Why can't you keep your dick in your pants? Why do you have to ruin everything?"

My dad asked me if I was done.

No, I said, I was not done. I don't even remember what words came out of my mouth next. My mind went black, my rage taking over.

When I finally took a breath, my dad jumped in. He told me I was still a little girl. A spoiled, sheltered little girl living in my little-girl world where I didn't know what real life was all about. He told me I didn't know how marriages worked or what was going on with his marriage and that I shouldn't know what was going on with his marriage because it was none of my business.

I told him it was my business because I loved Shellee. He made it my business when he brought Shellee into my life and made me love her, and now he was going to take her away, too.

"Don't come home for Christmas," he said, with the holiday still a month away. He didn't want me to cause a scene in front of Marshal.

"My mom just died!" I told him. "Where am I supposed to go?"

He told me to figure it out for myself. "You need to grow up," he said, then hung up.

I went back to Hawai'i that Christmas anyway; Shellee had asked me to. I didn't say anything to Marshal, then sixteen, keeping our chats to our shared tastes in metal bands and letting him show me what he was learning on the drums. Nor did I talk about it much with twenty-one-year-old Kalani, outside of a quick "What do you think is going to happen?" since Shellee had told him what was going on (he wasn't sure, either). I didn't say much to my dad at all. We exchanged presents and sat down for dinner, but otherwise, my dad hid away in his office, where he now slept.

Unlike all the other times when my dad and I got into a fight and would return for more words, more fire, this time, we didn't talk. We wouldn't see each other for over a year.

Ben, though, I was surprisingly still talking to. I crawled into his bed after work. We went on little dates to the Dresden and restaurants tucked in the canyon, trying to pretend things were normal. He was still obsessed with the Iowa college football team and was thrilled they had made it to the Orange Bowl the January that I came back after spending Christmas in Hawai'i. We didn't get tickets, but he needed to watch the game and place oranges around his television set and lay out jerseys and other team paraphernalia across the room, as if it was a seance. I bought takeout and tried to engage him in conversation about weekend plans and coworker gossip, but he remained focused on the television screen. Even when I kissed behind his ear, he was not interested. The Hawks were down, and he needed to focus all his attention on them.

"Goddammit!" he screamed when they officially lost. He paced around the living room, his brow furrowed. He was more distraught than I had ever seen him. I suggested we get out of the apartment and grab a drink. He chose the lounge of some lesser-known chain restaurant where highlights of the game played on high-definition screens around us. I asked him again about plans for the weekend, but I was mostly ignored. He huffed and puffed. The more he sulked, the more I couldn't stop thinking about my mother. *Why the hell am I consoling you over a fucking football game?* I could have taken my cue hours ago to call it a night and return to my bed alone. But I sat there, annoyed, resentful that his team's loss was the worst thing that had ever happened to him.

I kept returning to what my friend told me in Borders: I wanted to feel connected, if not to *everything*, at least to more things. I reached out to Claire, who suggested we go on an excursion to someplace new. We went farther west than our regular Hollywood Hills hikes, past the 405, toward Pacific Palisades to Sullivan Canyon. It was quieter there. No designer leggings or chunky highlights in sight. As we trudged past wildflowers and walked the dusty trail, we talked about what auditions she'd been on; I told her how I planned to open my journal again, soon. We commiserated about how the guys we were dating seemed not quite right for us—hers was too intense, mine not intense enough. Then she turned to me, with care in her eyes, and asked the simple question, "How are you feeling?" I stopped midstep and looked at her. Tears started rolling down my face. She put her arm around me, my wet cheeks in the neck of her shirt. "Fucked up," I told her. "I don't know how to make it stop." We stood there for a minute as she held me, the sun peeking through the shade of the trees, warming our backs.

When we got back to the car, she grabbed an old receipt from the floor and wrote a name and number on it. "This is my therapist," she said. "Take it." I gave her a skeptical look. "It's LA, Jessica—everyone has a therapist," she said. We laughed, and I took the paper from her outstretched hand. I knew I had to start believing my father was wrong: I had much more in life than myself.

I also thought about Shellee's suggestion to get away. The therapist seconded this idea, which didn't mean jumping in the car and embarking on a barhopping bender in a new town but going somewhere to be in the moment, alone. I started researching inns along the California coast, nothing too far, settling on a small hotel in Santa Barbara for five days. The morning I was supposed to leave, I gave myself errands to run until midafternoon, thinking if I left at 2:00, maybe 2:30, then at least half the day would be over by the time I got there. I packed my car with clothes, books, my stereo, my sad CDs, my pensive CDs, and a brand-new journal. I pulled out of my driveway, windows down, radio blasting, before I drove a whole block and stopped to buy a pack of cigarettes.

When I finally got to Santa Barbara, I thought I'd ease myself into alone time with a walk down the tourist-crowded State Street. I told myself to look away from my watch and at what was in front of my face instead: a woman in big sunglasses; a crushed Coke can on the ground. I started to think about where I could eat dinner, how much money I should spend, which night I'd let myself splurge on a fancy meal. I shook my head and kept on moving.

I spotted a coffee shop near the ocean and decided to make that my destination. I sat down with a latte, a muffin, and my journal. I thought I'd warm up to the journaling process by giving myself a task: make a list of what I wanted to do during this trip. *Read, hike, write.* I put my pen down and looked at a couple of college kids giggling over a triangle of blueberry pie. I pulled my head back to my page. *Pay attention to what you're doing.* I added it to my list. I jotted a few more vague phrases and sentences, including, *Don't put your pen down again for fifteen minutes.* Three pages later, I was writing about the fake me, the real me, and who cared about all those versions of me. Did I care? I took a breath. I grabbed my stuff and walked out the door. Twenty feet later, I stopped at a bench and filled two more pages.

Later that evening, I walked to the pier downtown. I thought about my dad escorting me on my move to LA. How when we were hungry or bored, he always ended up driving us back to Santa Monica. As we ate lunch at a clam joint near the pier, the scurry of plates bustling around us, he mentioned he could hear the water crashing onto the shore. My father never liked to be too far from the ocean.

Here, ninety miles away from Santa Monica and on a different boardwalk, I paused to watch the water splash over the planks' edges on the Santa Barbara pier. In the distance, waves rolled in, cresting, the flip of their whitewash smoothing out, then spreading across the sand. The steady rhythm of water receding back into the mass of blue before breaking, stretching, and receding once again. All this movement is meditative; there's a reason "ocean sounds" are a popular sleep aid, I thought. But it's also reenergizing to watch each ripple wash in and out, cleanse and return, one following another.

I turned from the water and walked toward a man in a funky white fedora playing "The Girl from Ipanema" on his saxophone. As he hit each bouncy note, the wrinkles around his eyes deepened. Every few lines, he took a short breath. A sandy-haired kid, egged on by his parents, came up and dumped pennies into the case at the musician's feet. A few seconds later, one half of an elderly couple stumbled over a plank; the other caught him by the arm. By the end of the song, two gawky teens were spinning one another to the bossa nova beat.

For five whole minutes, I forgot I had nowhere to go.

Most years, over a million people visit Pele's home. When she is erupting, you can see rivers of bright-red lava flowing from the crater to the ocean, cooling to become new land. At night, this black earth glows red from within, Pele's fire moving, shifting, and settling to illuminate the darkness.

When Pele is really pissed, you are not allowed to roam the Hawai'i Volcanoes National Park. Her lava is wild, spitting up like geysers when it hits the water, emitting a plume of volcanic gas that makes it hard to breathe and instigating earthquakes that rattle the homes of nearby residents.

But on a calm day when Pele is at peace, you can take several small hikes through the park's more than three hundred thousand acres. Its national park designation was established in 1916 after great pressure from Lorrin Thurston—the grandson of an influential missionary; a lead voice in the overthrow of the Hawaiian monarchy; and the owner of the local newspaper, which ran endorsements from President Roosevelt to have Pele's sacred 'āina fall under government jurisdiction. One of the more popular features of the park is the five-hundred-year-old lava tube named after Thurston but more commonly known to the Kānaka as Nāhuku. The underground passageway that once transported lava was a place of refuge for the Hawaiians, much like the one where Pele learned to harness her kuleana and where her 'ohana sheltered themselves from Kamapua'a's terror.

Another popular attraction is the steam vents at Kīlauea's summit, where groundwater seeps down into the heated rocks and spews back out as steam. Tourists often snap pictures of themselves standing in front of the sulfur banks, a smelly steam cloud rising behind them, looking somewhat like a fart. This steam, though, is not just sectioned off like a zoo animal or good for Facebook jokes. You can find it in the rain forests of Puna, evidence of Pele's mana, her life force. Even when she is not erupting, her breath is always around us.

But what is perhaps most impressive is what you can't see yet. In anywhere from five to fifty years, the ground that Pele burned, and the ground that she created, will be ready for new growth. Mineral-rich ash nourishes the soil. Layers of algae and mosses give way to native 'ama'u ferns, the little fingers of their fronds curling in the sun. Hi'iaka is always standing by, ready to lend a hand to cultivate fresh life.

Over the year I didn't talk to my father, Shellee slowly forgave him. She told me they started going to church together and began couples counseling. I tried not to interfere; my therapist told me not to. I had my own grieving to do.

Then, one November day, a year after my mom died, my dad called me out of the blue. He wanted to come up and visit. I was too curious to say no. He told me his flight information, but I didn't offer to pick him up from the airport, and he didn't ask. A few weeks later, there he was on my doorstep at sunset, just as he said he'd be. He was carrying a cooler filled with kalua pig, cabbage, lomi lomi salmon, and poi. The fixings for a lūʻau.

I stepped out of the way and let him in. He took off his slippers. "You remember Mong, right?" I asked, motioning to my roommate, who was sitting on the couch in our new Daniel-less apartment east of Hollywood. They nodded at each other.

"I figured you and I were probably going out for dinner," I said, eyeing Mong, then the cooler.

"No worries," my dad said. "I brought plenny."

My dad headed straight for the kitchen. I staggered between stepping in his direction or back toward the couch. "Need anything?" I asked.

"No, I think I got it," he called out.

I rejoined Mong on the couch. "Um, this is kinda weird, right?" I whispered.

She shrugged. "I dunno, it's actually kinda cool," she said. "I haven't had Hawaiian food in so long."

I heard the click of the gas stove being lit. The cold pork sizzled as it hit the pan. The smell of smoky pig wafted its way across the ceiling of our living room.

"Damn, that smells good," Mong said.

I could hear my dad opening up the cupboards, looking for some kind of seasoning. I jumped off the couch.

"Looking for something?"

"Found it," he said, raising the bottle of shoyu.

"Here." He threw me a handful of wooden chopsticks from his bag. "You can set da table," he said with a grin.

My dad dished the kalua and cabbage out of the pan and put the container of store-bought lomi lomi salmon on the table. He found a bowl to pour the bag of poi into. Then he brought over the sugar bowl. I'm what you call a "cheater," someone who likes to add sugar to my poi.

We all picked up our chopsticks and began rummaging through the mounds on our plates. The pig was juicy, the acid of the tomato and onion in the lomi a nice balance to its fattiness. My dad also made sure to add the right amount of water to the poi to get it the perfect consistency, neither too dense nor too runny. Aloha ran through every bite.

"This is so good," Mong said, breaking the silence. I nodded.

For the rest of dinner, my dad listened as we took turns making small talk about our jobs, interjecting to ask questions about the traffic and where things were in LA.

"How's your car holding up?" he asked me.

"Fine."

"Maybe we should take it fo' a tune-up while I'm hea."

"I think it's OK," I said, shoveling a hunk of pork into my mouth. "I got an oil change a month ago, and everything was fine."

He nodded. "OK."

The next day my father called from his hotel, asking what I wanted to do. I told him I was trying to get outdoors more often. It wasn't lost on me how ridiculous it was to move away from a place screaming in vegetation and rainbows, only to find nature in a city known for artifice and smog.

My dad picked me up in his rental, and we drove to the bottom of Griffith Park. Before we set out on our hike, he stretched for a few minutes, preparing to take his body, stiff from thirty-five years of manual labor, for a jaunt to the observatory. This was the first time the two of us did something outdoors and physical together since my failed summer work at the nursery. Our heavy panting up the mountain didn't allow either of us to say much. We talked little about Shellee and their marriage, other than him saying he loved her. But it was nice to walk side by side, just focusing on where to step in the dirt.

As we made our final descent back toward the parking lot, my dad said he wanted to stop and stretch again. He walked over to a lone park bench and propped his foot on it. He bent his head over his calves, his narrow back extended over his knees. I was usually in too much of a rush to stretch, but since I was there, I bent over and let my head hang toward the earth. I watched my father reach for his toes. He could almost do it. Almost. "Old bones," he said, putting his foot back on the ground.

As we walked to the car, he turned his face toward mine. "I'm sorry I left your mother."

I almost skipped a step. "Huh?"

"She deserved better den dat."

His words radiated in my ear—*den dat.* I looked at him, surprised he was talking about my mom and not his more recent indiscretion. Maybe the long-ago past was easier to address than the present. I nodded, satisfied with the lack of clarity. We kept walking to the car.

Epilogue

At takeoff, whether it's back to Los Angeles or New York, where I now live, I think of the lyrics to "Honolulu City Lights." "Looking out into the city night" from my window, the plane moving away from the clusters of light and into the scattered clouds, I know that I won't be back soon enough. I can hear the grief in Keola Beamer's voice as he repeats, "And it's not easy to leave again," holding on to that *eeeeeasy* for as long as he can.

It's another sad song I listened to in high school, one written by Beamer that he performed with his brother Kapono at the tail end of the Hawaiian Renaissance. Keola was planning a trip to California, the beginning of many travels for the brothers, who would play this melody all over the world. "I'm a Hawaiian through and through, and it's difficult to leave the place you love," he once said.

It's been over twenty years since I moved away, and whenever I'm back in Oʻahu, I spend a good portion of my trip noting how much I appreciate the eye smiles and nods hello of passersby on the sidewalk, on a run, in line at the fish market. Oh, how I've missed the double-cheek kisses of friends I haven't seen in months or years, and yet we can pick up right where we left off over karaage pūpū and Asahis. It is not lost on me that aloha is, indeed, never in short supply. And then I always wonder, *Should I move back?* I haven't yet, though. I still make the same excuses about my career, plus now I have a husband and a child to consider, too.

But these excuses don't stop my eyes from welling up as soon as I feel the air, so warm and embracing, when I step off the plane. Nor do they prevent me from wanting to hug the sound of slippers smacking against the ground. Coming home is a long exhale.

After my papa passed and my brothers were all grown, my dad and Shellee moved out of Kalihi. My father wanted to give his wife what she'd always wanted—land to farm on the windward side, in Waimānalo. On these thirty acres, they grow papaya, avocado, lemon, 'ulu, and cacao. Behind their home are the Ko'olaus in full regalia. I may not have noticed the cliffs behind us in Kalihi or the ocean view from my mother's yard in Makakilo, but it's impossible to miss the Ko'olaus, dripping in green, the clouds grazing their tip-tops.

My son is obsessed with them, too. "Where are the mountains?" he asks when we are at the beach. "Behind you," I tell him. In Hawai'i, you can orient yourself by whether you are ma uka (mountainside) or ma kai (oceanside); if one is in front of you, the other is always behind.

Even though I may question whether it makes sense for my little 'ohana to pack up everything we own and live in the middle of the ocean, my nonlocal family is wowed by Hawai'i. My husband is a surfer, an outdoorsman; it is not a coincidence that I found a partner who inspires me to go outside and hike a mountain or jump in the water when I still have the inclination to hole up in front of the television to decompress. My son loves to be around his cousins—Kalani, his wife, and their three kids live twenty minutes away from the farm, where Marshal also occasionally lends a hand. My son loves his grandma Shellee, asking her questions about the chickens she's raising or the "dinosaur egg" lychee that grows in the shade. In the circles they walk around the farm or as they sit playing dump trucks, she gives him that undivided attention she gave me when I needed it most. These days, she eats up his enthusiastic ramblings about errant boars and chicken poop, too.

My father died a few years back; he ended up with Alzheimer's like his mother and Uncle Mano. Despite his tendency toward anger and his fierce independence, the illness did not cause my dad to double down into his strongest personality quirks like it did to them. He was sweet, docile. He signaled with his big brown eyes that he was listening, even when the words would not come out. In the early days of his illness, he let me take him on walks through Waikīkī and up to the pillboxes on Kaʻiwa Ridge above Kaʻōhao, near Kailua. We sat side by side on beach chairs near the lagoon behind the Hilton, sipping on piña coladas like we did when we played tourists during my college days. These were things I wanted to do, and he was happy to oblige. As his illness progressed, what brought him joy and purpose was taking care of a collection of plants he had purchased from the neighborhood nursery. Digging in the dirt was in his muscle memory, the ʻāina in his blood.

With both of my parents gone and having lived away for so long, I've often returned to the question: How much do I belong in Hawaiʻi? In my decades away, I've become aware, painfully at times, of all that I missed about the islands, even when I was still living there. I've sought a deep connection with my ancestors' history. I listened to aloha ʻāina warriors and those who've spent their lives caring for the land. I continue to learn ʻōlelo and take hula lessons so that I can pass these traditions on to my son. While I may not live in Hawaiʻi or look or act a certain way, I will always be a local girl. I never feel more vulnerable than when I am in the islands—under the sun, aloha woven in the winds—and for that, I am so grateful.

One of my favorite things to do, besides immediately buying a meat jun plate from Gina's and shoving egg-battered fried meat and mac salad into my mouth, is to wander into the ocean alone. I often go to Kaimana's in Waikīkī, the beach of local townies who just like to lie in the sun and wade in the water. I swim out until I can barely touch the bottom. Facing the coastline, I can see the flamingo pink of the Royal Hawaiian hotel, the booze-cruise catamarans parked on the sand in front of the Outrigger, all the new and old hotels lining the shore, and I think of having poke at the Chart House at the other end of Waikīkī with my dad, the two of us gazing out into the harbor. Then I close my eyes and just feel the current. The rise and fall of the small waves bobbing me around. I have to trust that the ocean won't send me a push that my body can't handle. I can feel the sun on me, the mana reaching my naʻau, and I cry. I cry until I am ready to return to shore.

FURTHER READING

Voices of Fire, by kuʻualoha hoʻomanawanui, is a thorough examination of Pele and Hiʻiaka moʻolelo, put into cultural and historical context from the Kanaka perspective. With hula performances restricted and Hawaiian language banned for nearly a hundred years, Pele moʻolelo, up until recently, has mostly been reduced to cutesy fables for Western consumption. hoʻomanawanui, though, breaks down what Pele and Hiʻiaka moʻolelo mean not only to Hawaiian values but also cultural survival. "Together, Pele and Hiʻiaka represent aloha ʻāina through their symbiotic (pono, ʻēkoʻa) roles as creator and regenerator of the ʻāina," she writes. Through great detail and thoughtful analysis, hoʻomanawanui makes clear not only her authority in honoring these moʻolelo, but also her kuleana: of this work, she writes, "I did not choose it, it chose me."

In *Pau Hana*, historian Ronald Takaki digs deeper than the abbreviated, happy-ending history of how "the plantation days" resulted in Hawaiʻi becoming one big melting pot. Written in 1983, the book takes into account the journals and records of plantation owners and laborers and includes interviews of those who lived through it. The result is a comprehensive history of immigration and race relations in the islands through the mid-1900s—one that, yes, helped form what we think of today as "local" identity but was also much more complicated than plantation workers swapping lunches and speaking Pidgin.

Local Story, by University of Hawai'i associate history professor John P. Rosa, details the Massie–Kahahawai case, another big turning point for defining local identity in Hawai'i. Much like the plantations illustrated the power of white settlers (haole) and the oppression of everyone else (Kānaka, immigrants brought in for labor), this case exposed the reach white foreigners had in the islands, from the backing of the US military to the way they were heralded as either victims or saviors in the media. While the Massie–Kahahawai case has been the focus of numerous true-crime books and television movies, played up for a salacious assault-and-murder plot in "paradise," Rosa sticks to the facts, using police statements, media coverage, geographical context, and local and American responses to the trial's outcome to paint a mosaic of racial and socioeconomic injustice in the islands.

In *Hawaiian Blood*, J. Kēhaulani Kauanui explains the far-reaching impacts of blood-quantum laws in Hawai'i. As Kauanui writes, "Blood quantum is a manifestation of settler colonialism that works to deracinate—to pull out by the roots—and displace indigenous people." She lays out how the US government not only forcibly took the Kānaka's land but also felt entitled to determine who was Native Hawaiian and then allowed a number of those "aboriginals" to apply for small parcels of land accordingly. But perhaps just as significant, by asserting that Hawaiian blood was "absorbed" into whiteness, the haole elite attempted to make Kānaka believe that what was left of their identity was insignificant, shaping how generations of Hawaiians have since seen themselves.

Nā Kua'āina, by Davianna Pōmaika'i McGregor, is an antidote to the suppression of Hawaiian culture. McGregor, a founding member of the University of Hawai'i's Ethnic Studies Department, examines five rural regions in the islands and how their way of life is shaped by tradition—from the taro grown in Waipiʻo to the devotion of Pele in Puna. While these areas haven't been untouched by Westernization, they remain steeped in cultural practices through communities coming together to revitalize activities and stand up for the ʻäina.

ACKNOWLEDGMENTS

This book would have never seen the light of day without my incredible agent, Lauren Abramo, who took great care in guiding my proposal, and my editors, Laura Van der Veer and Tenyia Lee, who saw the connective tissue between a dozen tangentially related ideas and helped me make sense of it all. I'm also indebted to Davianna Pōmaika'i McGregor for bringing clarity to my gaps in Hawaiian history and to Pua Aki for offering thoughtful notes about language and cultural sensitivities. Big thanks to Kirsten Balayti for her careful copyediting eye, Karen Parkin for her close read, and Emma Reh and everyone else at Little A who helped usher this book along.

Nothing on the page would exist, though, if not for my mentor and friend Debra Gwartney, who helped me believe I was a writer. Much of this book started with her showing me what a memoir should look like. Thanks also to my generous friend Julia Holmes, who offered incisive notes on my drafts and the gift of uninterrupted space to write.

There are also my everyday cheerleaders, the people who have always pushed me to keep on: my parents, whom I still miss every day; my Shellee, who always made me believe what I had to say was cool and interesting, even if it wasn't; my brothers, Kalani, Marshal, and Tom, who've shown me I'm not alone; my forever friends Melanie, Becca, Mong, Farrah, Riyo, Sean, Ele, Andrea, Aaron, Jessica, Barbara, Megan, Carly, and Marisa for offering me light; my mom's friends Darlene and

Steve, who have kept her loving spirit alive; and my Harshings group text, who kept me laughing as I wrote this thing in a pandemic. Most of all, mahalo nui loa to my husband, Chris, who was supportive of me squeezing in hours and days away to write and who didn't run when I gave him a draft of this manuscript when we first met. And my son, Leo, who makes me want to live the lessons I learned writing this book.

ABOUT THE AUTHOR

Photo © 2022 Jena Cumbo

Jessica Machado is an editor at NBC News. Previously, she was a staff editor at Vox, the Daily Dot, and *Rolling Stone*. Her work has appeared in the *Washington Post*, the Cut, BuzzFeed, Vice, and *Elle*, among others. Born and raised in Hawaiʻi, she currently lives in Brooklyn, New York. For more information, visit www.jessica-machado.com.